OLD ENGLISH VILLAGES

OLD ENGLISH VILLAGES

✤ Clay Perry ✤

TEXT BY
Ann Gore ✤ Laurence Fleming

Weidenfeld and Nicolson   London

Acknowledgments

We would like to thank all those members of the Women's Institutes who have, so very kindly, sent us the most interesting material about their villages. Also, our grateful thanks to Miss Edna Rylands, Mrs Halsey Colchester, Mr Richard Rowland and Mr William Gore for their help in disinterring the history of various villages throughout England.

L.F. and A.G.

Text copyright © Ann Gore and Laurence Fleming 1986
Photographs copyright © George Weidenfeld & Nicolson Ltd 1986
Photographic Notes copyright © Clay Perry 1986

First published in 1986 by
George Weidenfeld & Nicolson Ltd
91 Clapham High Street, London SW4 7TA

Designed by Joy FitzSimmons

Colour separations by Newsele Litho Ltd
Filmset by Keyspools Ltd, Golborne, Lancashire
Printed and bound in Italy by L.E.G.O. Vicenza

Half Title Page Monks Eleigh, Suffolk
Title Page Swinbrook, Oxfordshire

❖ CONTENTS ❖

✦ INTRODUCTION ✦

Mincing Hampton,
Painswick Proud,
Beggarly Bisley,
Strutting Stroud.

So runs a local rhyme of the
towns and villages in the
Stroudwater area of the
Cotswolds. However, there
does not seem to have been
anything beggarly about Bisley
in the Middle Ages – or indeed
later, to judge by the amount
of interesting and solid houses
in and around the village, such
as Jaynes Court, Wesley
House, Over Court, which was
once the property of Queen
Elizabeth I, and many others.

The hazy mist is lifting now, out of the shallow valley. Against the line of silver willows the cows stand still, knee-deep in buttercups, waiting for the sun to warm their backs. In the same meadow, nearer the village, two horses look over a gate that is flanked by high hedges, lately burdened by the May blossom but now with a froth of Queen Anne's lace at their feet. Far off, a clock strikes five. A cock crows, a door bangs, hasty footsteps on the soft mud road, a man moving out of the village with a scythe on his back, four miles to walk to work today. A white file of plump ducks ambles across to the pond, quacking with anticipation. In the yard behind the farmhouse overlooking the green the hens begin to chatter, the horses to stamp impatiently in the straw. In the smithy beyond the superb chestnut, now in flower, a sound of bellows, a clink of metal, can be heard. The scents of yesterday, a field of clover, some new-mown hay, still linger. Only the yews in the churchyard stand sombre. Then the air is filled with the warm, delicious smell of bread taken hot from the oven. An English village is awake.

Perhaps at no time in its long history has the English village been quite like this, it is only the reflection, the romantic recollection, the village of Christmas cards, calendars and advertisements for beer. But the dream-village nevertheless lies close to the surface of the English mind; to live in a village in the calm of the English countryside is, for many, the ambition of their lives.

Villages have suggested patterns to successful town planners of the past, the urban square of houses round a communal garden; the terraces, offering the kind of contact to be found in rows of cottages straggling down a village street. Even the great urban mass that is London may be regarded as a number of medieval and Tudor villages joined by, for instance, a seventeenth-century housing scheme, Soho, an eighteenth-century one, Bloomsbury, or a nineteenth-century one, Belgravia. Only the City of London was built as a city. Even the twentieth century, which has, in effect, joined Brentford to Braintree and Barnet to Beckenham, has not entirely obliterated the original flavour of these places.

English villages are all unique, the products of circumstances individual to each one. There is no pigeon-holing them, except in the loosest way. There are villages built round a green; there are villages not built round a green. There are villages strung along a valley, on a hill, in a dale, beneath a down, within a fold, along a road or at a crossroads. There are villages sited on very ancient Iron Age homesteads, within boundaries laid down thousands of years ago in the Bronze Age and – for some hundreds of years – within sound of the same church bell.

They were originally engaged in producing food; though they may later have come to make buttons, needles, pins or straw hats, agriculture was the base of their existence. They were small enough for everyone to know everyone else by face and name, to know if they were well or ill or, in an ancient phrase, 'if they had come up missing'.

They have been threatened, by civil wars, disease, hunger and enclosures; they have disappeared, beneath the plough, under the grassland, into the forest, under a reservoir. But they have survived; there are still some thirteen thousand villages in England. They have survived because the people who built them, and who have lived in them over the centuries, have adapted them, and have adapted with them, to the prevailing conditions; because they faced their enemies in common and, if they did not unite, they fell. There are some thirteen hundred lost villages in England.

The overwhelming charm of English villages lies in the fact that hardly any of them have been planned. They grew, larger or smaller, as circumstances demanded. Some, notably in the far north of England, were planned as early as the twelfth century to be centred on a rectangular green; but the houses that are there today were built at different times so regimentation has been avoided.

Planners like straight lines and segments of circles, not for them the Celtic curve or the subtleties of asymmetry, which are the principal components of the village as a composition. The English village does not impose itself upon the landscape. It accepts the lie of the land and the natural hazards with equanimity and, over the years, landscape and village have grown together.

For every fifty farmworkers in 1900 there are now perhaps seven. Their cottages, which should be empty, have been floored and given damp-courses, re-roofed, plumbed and painted, filled with stripped pine and Spanish rugs, to be visited at the weekend only. But they are there.

So – the old school lies silent, waiting to be awakened on Friday evening and put to sleep again on Sunday. The smart couple in the newly converted barn drive swiftly past in their Mercedes, en route for London seventy miles away, a journey they accomplish every working day. In the Old Rectory, the Admiral's widow, awake all night, lies sweetly asleep, lulled by the soothing tones of an early morning news reader. Very old George, an early riser always, cycles past on his way to the allotments. The General's widow, whose thatched house was once three labourer's cottages, is drawing back her chintz curtains. The new owner of the Manor House, a cattle dealer, leaves, a little late, on his forty-mile journey to today's market. A motor cycle roars, piloted by an engineer's draughtsman from the council houses, with twenty miles to go to work. There is the clink of milk bottles being delivered, the busy scuttle of the mail van stopping and starting through the village. Children, still chomping toast and cornflakes, gather for the school bus. An English village is alive.

✤ THE VILLAGE ✤

HALLATON, LEICESTERSHIRE

The church of St Michael at Hallaton is one of the most imposing village churches in Leicestershire, ranging in style from Norman to Decorated with a great west tower built in the thirteenth century. In the porch is the tympanum from the former Norman doorway – a spirited depiction of St Michael slaying the dragon with three small figures sheltering behind his shield. Hallaton was formerly a quite important small market town since it lies at the junction of five country roads; it now seems very remote although there are still plenty of interesting houses dating from the seventeenth to the nineteenth centuries. On a magnificent site about half a mile away are the grassy earthworks that are all that remain of Hallaton Castle, which was a Norman fortification built to protect an iron-working site.

Very few village buildings still standing today are older than the fifteenth century. Some manor houses and parsonages may be earlier than that, being substantially built, but the houses of farmers and labourers would not have been constructed to last. The oldest building in a village is nearly always the church – a village without a church being a hamlet – and it was the church that fixed the position of the village. Originally sited, in Saxon times, on some previous place of worship, it would have been in the centre of the village. Where a church now stands isolated, it is the village that has moved away, either of its own free will or as the deliberate action of a landlord. Often villages grew away from the church towards the south, or were clustered against the southern wall of the churchyard, seeking the sun as one might suppose; but there is a theory that, as the northern part of the churchyard was used for the burial of suicides and the unbaptized, no one wished to overlook it.

Many villages stand within territories that were defined in the Bronze Age, that is to say more than three thousand years ago, when England is thought to have had a higher population than when it was first recorded, in Domesday Book of 1086. It seems probable that these divisions survived into the Roman era, were accepted by the Saxons and were finally codified, as parishes, by the early medieval Church. Certain parishes had sections within other parishes, even as late as the eighteenth century, and it is possible that these may have been, for instance, areas for summer grazing or woodland for keeping pigs, from very ancient times indeed.

Some 250 churches in England are partly Saxon, that is to say founded before the Norman Conquest in 1066. They are nearly all made of stone, sometimes brought with enormous labour, by barge and cart, into districts where stone was not plentiful. Since the great cost of building the church was borne principally by the Lord of the Manor, we may suppose that stones rejected by the masons may have gone into the building of the Manor House, if not into the walls, at least into the foundations.

The ground for the church had to be given either by the lord or by the villagers themselves. In the Iron Age, the eight hundred years before the birth of Christ, the villagers are known to have held their land in common and to have shared their produce. Perhaps some of this communal ownership still existed; possibly it was what later came to be called 'common land'. When the old Saxon estates were being turned into parishes, one of the conditions was that the lord had to make provision for a priest. He gave the land for a house and frequently had to build the house as well, the property thenceforth belonging to the Church and being called 'glebe land'.

The system of tithing began under the Saxons, as long ago as AD 786, and was subsequently taken over by the Normans. This defined the parish even further since it ordained that everyone within the parish had to pay one tenth of his income – a tithe – to the Church, either in money or goods. Most village boundaries, however ancient in fact, were made official at this time and exist to this day. The tithe system, after much use and abuse, was not finally abolished until 1936.

The Saxon social system was also accepted, regularized and enforced by the Norman kings, and is known to us as the Feudal System. Under the Saxons it was quite rigid; there was the lord, his agent or reeve, a craftsman class of free peasants called *folgere*, who were paid for their labours, and an extremely complicated system of other peasants, at the bottom of which were the slaves or bondmen. Those who held their land from their lord – and there was no other way of obtaining it – did so on various conditions, including compulsory military service and a clearly defined quantity of forced labour. The Normans, who freed the slaves, amalgamated the peasant classes under the name of *villein*.

So the village hierarchy was founded very early, and with the later addition of the parson, was to continue more or less in this form until the end of the Second World War. The Feudal System itself gradually fell apart, disappearing completely by the beginning of the seventeenth century. The *villeins* separated into independent farmers, tenant farmers and smallholders; the craftsmen remained independent and perhaps became merchants; while the residue from all these classes formed a very vulnerable working class, with nothing to sell but their labour.

Conditions of life in Norman England were not easy. A *villein* could be fined if he married outside the village. He could be fined if he joined the Church without permission or if he sheltered a stranger. He was obliged to use the lord's mill to grind his corn, and to pay for it; he could be fined for keeping a hand mill at home. At his death, his lord took his best beast and the Church his second best. At the same time he

SMARDEN, KENT

Smarden lies in the Weald of Kent, on the river Beult, more or less in the centre of that rich farming country that owed its medieval prosperity to sheep. The entire county is scattered with buildings; there are practically no large tracts of uninhabited land. One of the causes of this 'high density' population is the old system of land tenure peculiar to Kent and known as *gavelkind*. Instead of the eldest son inheriting everything, the estate was divided equally between all the sons. 'Every son is as great a gentleman as the eldest son.' In general practice before the Conquest, *gavelkind* was suppressed by the Normans but was not finally abolished until 1922. It persisted only in Kent, and there are therefore far more houses for 'yeomen farmers' there than in the rest of the country. A particular style known as the 'Wealden house' was evolved to suit them.

had certain rights on common or waste land. He had the right to collect wood (*estover*) and to dig peat (*turbary*) for fuel; to collect timber for gates and fences (*heybote*), for repairing ploughs and carts (*plowbote*) and for building houses (*housebote*); above all, he had the right to fish (*piscary*). These rights, if exercised, must frequently have made the difference between survival and starvation. His house would have been dark, damp and insanitary, made of mud, branches and straw, and requiring to be entirely rebuilt about every twenty years.

Domesday Book did not list villages, as these were of a very impermanent nature. The landscape it describes consisted of isolated farmhouses and small groups of cottages. It records who held the land before the Normans came, whether it was arable, pastureland or woodland, how many people lived on it, and what tools they had. The point of comparison was 'T.R.E.' – *tempus regis Edwardi* – the time of King Edward the Confessor, the last Saxon king to die in his bed.

The weather at this time seems to have been particularly good. In the thirteenth century a crop failure would occur perhaps only once in twenty years. By 1250 the population is thought to have approached five million, from well under two million recorded in Domesday Book. The winter of 1348–9 is known to have been particularly mild, as in that year the fleas that brought the bubonic plague to England did not hibernate, but continued to feed. We shall never know just how many people died in the Black Death, as it was romantically called, but it was a great many. With the consequent shortage of labour, many landlords put arable land down to grass and began to keep sheep. England grows some of the best grass in the world, producing some of the best sheep, and so gradually an enormous and highly profitable trade in wool and woollen goods grew up.

Now the village could begin to thrive, and houses to be more substantially built – in Somerset and the Cotswolds of the local stone, in East Anglia and Kent of the local brick. New churches were built and old ones added to, being given a new chancel or a new spire, or both. Farmers and wool merchants, making some money, left their houses in the village for larger ones, perhaps a little further down the street, or up the hill, or beyond the pond. Their old houses were occupied by less prosperous families, whose houses were then lived in by poorer villagers. This was to be the pattern of village occupancy through the years, though not until about 1850 can we really pretend that everyone was living in a weatherproof house. The Romans, who

LAVENHAM, SUFFOLK

The Guildhall at Lavenham was built in 1529 although, by then, the Suffolk wool trade was in decline. Ironically, this was partly due to the restrictive practices of the very Guild that built the hall, though the rise of the worsted wool industry in Norfolk certainly contributed. For some hundred years before this Lavenham had been one of the leading wool villages and its blue cloth, stamped with the *fleur de lys* trademark, was deservedly famous. This trademark was introduced by Flemish weavers, invited by Edward III to settle in England and divulge the secrets of their craft. In due course, the Guildhall became the Town Hall and then the town gaol. So poorly maintained was it at that time that prisoners could sometimes kick their way out through the crumbling walls; but it has since been beautifully restored.

perfectly understood the making of damp-courses, unfortunately took their secret with them.

Around 1450 it is now thought that the weather grew both colder and wetter, a cycle that was to last for some four hundred years. Crop failures became more common, though one might suppose that the demand for wool and woollen cloth would have correspondingly increased. At this time, however, England was devastated by one of the most dreadful civil wars in history, the charmingly titled Wars of the Roses, which lasted for thirty years from 1455–85. It was a series of conflicts that must have affected everyone, being savagely fought, often with foreign troops, over the entire country. Village houses were still flimsy and easily burnt down; growing crops are always vulnerable. The misery caused by these wars is awful to contemplate. On the battlefield of Tewkesbury, in 1471, it is said that every noble family in England left a representative, dead; many families became extinct from that moment. One result of the Wars of the Roses was, however, that much of the land passed into new ownership. New tenancies had to be negotiated, based more on money than on compulsory labour, and farmers, both independent and tenant, who were by now called yeomen, became a force to be reckoned with.

In the early sixteenth century, a new player appears on the village scene: the parson's wife. Until the Reformation the village priest, whether vicar or rector, would have been a monk appointed by the local bishop, abbot or prior or, *very* occasionally, by the local lord. Away from the discipline of the monastery, however, he sometimes fell into temptation. John Skelton, one of our more uninhibited poets – and at one time tutor to the future King Henry VIII – was ordained in 1498 and became rector of Diss in Norfolk a few years later. When adjured by his bishop to 'send his wife out through the door', he did so, but took her in again through the window. With the establishment of the Church of England, its clergy were allowed to marry, and the parson's wife would reach the zenith of her power in the nineteenth century.

With the Dissolution of the Monasteries, which began in 1536, the great Church estates passed into new ownership and the end of the Feudal System as a system may be said to date from this time, though serfdom is thought to have existed in remote districts into the seventeenth century. There has been movement, both up and down, between the classes ever since.

BLANCHLAND, NORTHUMBERLAND

The village of Blanchland is on the river Derwent, which here forms the county boundary between Northumberland and County Durham. Blanchland Abbey was founded in 1165 and continued until its dissolution in 1539. In 1752 the abbey and the village came into the hands of the Crewe trustees and it is they who laid out the model village. It was built to house the lead miners who worked on the nearby moors. The houses and cottages are built round an L-shaped enclosure with, in its centre, a memorial to Queen Victoria. On one side is the Georgian Lord Crewe Hotel and, on the north, the gatehouse of the old monastery.

One of the most satisfying things about English villages is that they are all different. A complicated geology leads to changes of scenery within relatively short distances. The early village houses were made out of the soil, of locally quarried stone, of bricks made of local clay, or of the local clay itself when all else failed. The villages seem to adapt themselves to the landscape, rarely conforming to any preconceived pattern.

In the far north of England, however, one may still find villages built round rectangular village greens, dating from the eleventh century. After the so-called 'harrying of the north' in 1069 – the total destruction of all villages and crops in the area by the armies of William the Conqueror – the villages were rebuilt, some forty years later, on this plan. But, if these planned villages were heard of in the south, the idea does not seem to have been accepted.

What many villages would have had at this time, and indeed still do, is a village green. Cockfield in Suffolk still has nine. The history of the village green is complicated and in many cases obscure, but many of them are certainly the descendants of the market greens of the twelfth century. Market grants were issued by the Crown to individual Lords of the Manor giving permission to hold weekly markets, and large open spaces were created for this purpose. Sometimes two hamlets were joined by such a green, becoming thenceforth one village and building their church together. The system of village markets does not seem to have survived beyond the fourteenth century. One may suppose that there were too many sellers and not enough buyers and, if the neighbouring villages were also holding markets on that day, there would have been very few buyers indeed. But if the markets failed, the greens remained, their rights jealously guarded by all concerned. The only building allowed on the village green was the communal well.

If there ever was a Merrie England – and modern research techniques are making this seem more and more unlikely – it could conceivably have been during the lifetime of William Shakespeare, who lived between 1564 and 1616. The wool trade had, in fact, collapsed around 1550 and the number of vagrants, who previously would have been cared for in the monasteries and convents, was so enormous that the first of the Poor Laws had to be passed. But the currency, twice devalued by King Henry VIII, had been called in and re-issued by his much shrewder daughter, Queen Elizabeth I, at a profit of £14,000 to herself. It was now on a much sounder basis.

MONKS ELEIGH, SUFFOLK

A village pump that tells its own story! It does, however, remind one how hard and primitive life was for the inhabitants of many of the villages in England right up to the middle of the twentieth century. This seems particularly true of East Anglia, parts of which are still very remote. Even a great house such as Felbrigg in Norfolk – now owned by the National Trust – had no electricity until after the 1940s.

Foreign money was coming into the country, either by trade or by force, the enemy of the time being Spain. 'The spreading chestnut tree', soon to enter village mythology, also arrived at this time, perhaps from Turkey as a conker in the pocket of a merchant trading in carpets.

The seventeenth century saw another great civil war, between 1642 and 1649, but the destruction seems to have been directed mostly towards the churches and cathedrals. Nearly all the medieval stained glass and most of the medieval statues were deliberately destroyed at this time. The villages themselves, now much more solidly founded and constructed, and in many cases no longer roofed with thatch, were by no means so easily put to fire and sword. The end of the century saw the draining of fens and marshes and an entirely new interest in both horticulture and agriculture among the country gentry. A new era for village dwellers seemed in prospect.

This was the time of 'Lady Bountiful', a person much maligned by modern social historians. She appeared in *The Beaux' Stratagem* in 1707, described by her creator, George Farquhar as 'an old, civil, Country Gentlewoman, that cures all her Neighbours of all distempers'. She makes remarks like: 'Well, good woman, go to the pantry, get your bellyful of victuals' and 'I have done miracles about the country here with my receipts', undoubtedly an ancestress of the modern welfare state.

The period between 1690 and 1830 was perhaps the greatest in English architecture, at all levels of society. It is rare to find a really ugly building dating from this time. In the villages, the squire possibly had additional income from abroad, perhaps from India or the West Indies, and, in particular, the parson had a new status. He is vividly described by Henry Fielding in 1742, in his novel *The Adventures of Joseph Andrews*, as being 'a parson on Sundays, but all the other six might be more properly called a farmer. He occupied a small piece of land of his own, besides which he rented a considerable deal more. His wife milked his cows, managed his dairy, and followed the markets with butter and eggs. The hogs fell chiefly to his care . . .' Lord Macaulay wrote, of the same period, that the clergy were 'regarded, on the whole, as a plebeian class . . . His boys followed the plough; and his girls went out to service'.

The country gentry, however, with a higher standard of living themselves, were having larger families, or rather, more of them were surviving infancy. Some respectable provision had to be made for the daughters and younger sons. From about 1730 it became acceptable for a young lady of good family to marry a parson, which would have been unthinkable in the seventeenth century, and frequently her dowry was spent on building a handsome new parsonage. Similarly it became acceptable for a younger son of the squire to become a parson, and he frequently acceded to, and held for his lifetime, a living that was in the gift of his father.

In 1752, William Halfpenny, 'architect and carpenter', published his *Useful Architecture in Twenty One New Designs for erecting Parsonage-houses, Farm-houses and Inns, with their respective Offices, &c, of Various Dimensions, at the most moderate Expence, the largest not exceeding Five Hundred Pounds, and the smallest under One Hundred Pounds*. The smallest was designed to be a parsonage or a farmhouse, the largest a parsonage only. Later in the century there was to be a great vogue for building Picturesque cottages but, while an astonished lodge-keeper, or an amazed gamekeeper, might find himself actually residing in one, they were not really intended as regular habitations and very few were included in ordinary villages.

An inn designed by an architect was as much of a novelty as William Halfpenny presumably intended. The ale-wife of the Middle Ages – and many villages had as many as three – had gradually been replaced over the years by hostelries of varying doubtfulness. The ale-wife was frequently a widow who supported herself by brewing her own beer and selling it from her own front door. It was available day and night. The first licensing laws date from 1872.

With a new parsonage built, the old one might be occupied by a farmer, or converted into a dower house for the young squire's widowed mother and his unmarried sisters, or 'elevated into a Cottage' for the newly married son of the squire. The gradual silting up of the poorer gentry into village houses provided alternative employment for the villagers as servants; and though stable boys continued to sleep in the hay loft into the present century, and housemaids slept in attics that were not always heated, it is probable that they were better fed and clothed than they would have been at home.

But the principal event of the eighteenth century, and the one that was to lead to the extinction of any kind of independence for the villager, was the gradual enclosing of the land. The medieval rights to gather wood on common land and to fish in common streams had lasted until this time. Now, by various private Acts of Parliament, the commons and waste lands were incorporated into the estates of the landowners. The woods and streams became private property; the collection of wood was now theft and the taking of fish, poaching. Poaching laws were particularly savage and man-traps were not made illegal until 1827.

The novels of Jane Austen give us pictures of several English villages at the turn into the nineteenth century. We find Emma, after a visit to a sick cottager, 'stopping to look once more at all the outward wretchedness of the place, and recall the still greater within'. We find Mrs Norris, in *Mansfield Park*, a parson's widow and sister of the squire's lady, fixing on 'the smallest habitation which could rank as genteel among the buildings of Mansfield parish, the White House being only just large enough to receive herself and her servants, and allow a spare room for a friend'. We find Lady Catherine de Bourgh, in *Pride and Prejudice*, who 'whenever any of the cottagers were disposed to be quarrelsome, discontented, or too poor . . . sallied forth into the village to settle their differences, silence their complaints, and scold them into harmony and plenty'.

Both Lady Catherine, of Rosings Park, and Sir Thomas Bertram, of Mansfield Park, lived in handsome modern buildings quite possibly in newly enclosed parkland, well out of sight of the village. Throughout the nineteenth century the upper gentry moved away from the village, the parson's wife taking the place of the squire's lady in the social order.

By 1840, the enclosures were complete. The villager depended for his livelihood entirely on his employment; all his rights in the land had gone and this was not even partially corrected until the Small Holdings and Allotments Act of 1908, which allowed people to rent land from the parish. Another Act of 1922 describes an allotment as being a piece of land 'which is wholly, or mainly, cultivated by the occupier for the production of vegetables and fruit crops for consumption by himself and his family'. Until then, he could supplement his wages only with what he could grow in his garden, if he had one.

But although the village labourer in the nineteenth century was almost as dependent on his employer as he had been in Saxon times, he was by no means quite so helpless, for there were now railways and steamships, also, as a rule, equipped with sails. Around 1850 the villages were overflowing with people and unpaid lay-offs were the terror of the villagers, because without work they starved. So they began to leave, to find work in the towns, to go to North America or to the Antipodes.

LONGSTOCK, HAMPSHIRE

With the building of motorways, Hampshire has become very accessible from London and many an old cottage has been converted into a 'gent's res'. The change in village life from full-time working occupants to weekenders and retired people can be deplored or welcomed, depending on the point of view. Cottages that might have fallen or been pulled down have now been lovingly restored, like this one. The tell-tale vent pipe poking up through the corner of the thatch hints at interior improvements in the shape of bathrooms. The staddle stones by the front door would have originally supported a grain store, the raised level being effective in keeping out rats.

In 1860, the countryside supported about two million farmers and labourers; by 1900 their number had been halved.

Two new characters now appear in the village: the policeman, who arrived in the mid-century, and the schoolteacher. There had always been schools in villages, though not by any means in every village, organized by the Church or by some philanthropic person. They were frequently run by women – the Dame Schools – and attendance was largely dictated by the state of the harvest, since children could earn pennies for scaring birds, or picking up stones, or weeding, or stooking, or gleaning. Someone also had to take Father his lunch and he could be two or three miles away. This situation continued even after the Education Act of 1870, which provided a school in each village. These have now been swept away and the children sent to super-schools. The village policeman has also been centralized, and mechanized, and may be miles away when some emergency occurs.

English agriculture reached a peak of prosperity around 1870 and it has been having ups and downs ever since. The First World War took away the men, as the long lists of war dead in the churches of quite tiny villages show. The village was to reach its lowest ebb in the years after that war, its produce undercut by cheaper Canadian wheat, and cheaper Australian wool, and cheaper New Zealand lamb. In the mid 1930s, the average wage was to fall to £1 16s a week, some £43 in today's money.

Now, the horse has been replaced by the tractor, which will accomplish in a day work that would have kept five plough teams busy for a week. It will also tackle very heavy soil previously unbroken by the plough. In a particular village in 1901, there were eight farmers, who employed forty-five men and kept thirty-five workhorses. In the same village in 1975, there were six farmers, six farm labourers, nineteen tractors and two combine harvesters. Less than three per cent of the population was employed in agriculture in that year, but they produced twice as much barley, three times as much wheat, twenty times as much sugar beet and four times as much pork and bacon as they were doing forty-five years before.

So today we have our villages, masterpieces of unplanning, spontaneously built by the people who lived in them over hundreds of years, rescued from oblivion by the motor car. The real cottage gardens have mostly gone – those wonderful collections of cabbages, cabbage roses, peas and stocks, mint and sage, broad beans, kidney beans, cauliflowers, Canterbury bells, hollyhocks, Madonna lilies, pinks and potatoes, all superbly healthy on their daily diet of night-soil. African marigolds, salvias and lobelias have rather taken over. But even now nothing is standard in an English village, not the church, nor the green, nor the gardens, and certainly not the people. Not long ago, a woman who had lived all her life in two neighbouring villages in Oxfordshire was heard to say, of a village in Gloucestershire less than five miles away: 'O, they're all very wild over there.'

If, in general, they do obey the one great English commandment – 'Thou shalt ignore thy neighbour as much as possible' – at least one can be sure that when threatened, by the local authority, or the Ministry of Defence, or the Ministry of Transport, or the local diocese, or the Ministry of Health, they will close their ranks and engage the foe.

Villagers are not as vulnerable as they were. Their houses are in better repair than ever before; their roads are no longer ankle deep in mud; they no longer depend on a good harvest for their holidays; or face serious misery with a fall in the price of wheat. They are tractor-drivers, lorry-drivers, mechanical engineers, painters and potters and hand-loom weavers, retired bank managers, whizz-kid executives, hairdressers, herdsmen, farmers and factory hands, schoolteachers, advertisers, redundant typographers, unsuccessful wheeler-dealers, writers to *The Times* . . . And therein lies their strength.

CLEY-NEXT-THE-SEA, NORFOLK

Cley-next-the-Sea is a small, very pretty village of brick and flint houses, which lies on a former estuary of the river Claven, opposite Wiveton. These two villages were important ports until the 1820s, when a bank was put across the estuary and Cley rapidly silted up. As early as 1580, Cley (pronounced Cly), Wiveton and Blakeney had between them more than twenty ships of more than fifty tons. Wiveton still had a ship-building industry in the seventeenth century. Cley's medieval quay was probably sited at the southern end of the churchyard where there is now a green. The old village was grouped here, but after the great fire of 1612, which destroyed or damaged 117 houses and buildings, it was rebuilt on a new site. The beautiful eighteenth-century windmill at the end of the quay has been converted into a private house.

CLEY-NEXT-THE-SEA, NORFOLK

These charming brick and flint cottages are typical of the architecture of north-eastern Norfolk. Norfolk has a foundation of chalk, but this lies close to the surface only in the north of the county, where it produces lime for mortar and the flints that are used as a building material throughout East Anglia. Sometimes the flint stones are used whole, as here, giving a 'pebbly' appearance; or they can be cut – knapped – giving a flatter surface and exposing their beautiful toffee-coloured centres. The walls are nearly always dressed at the corners and round the windows with local brick. Flemish craftsmen brought the art of making bricks to East Anglia in the fifteenth century. Timber is in short supply here and used sparingly. Records tell us that sawn timber from Sussex was being imported at Blakeney even in the sixteenth century.

LAXFIELD, SUFFOLK

Despite the advent of the supermarket and the enormous increase in car ownership, the small multi-purpose grocery still has an important part to play in village life. Often the Post Office and the shop are one but, unusually, at Laxfield the grocer and the draper are teamed together. In most small villages the shop forms part of a cottage but here, rather more grandly, it is a small house. This one is absolutely typical of the small 'gentry' houses to be found in almost all Suffolk villages. The pale brick, common throughout East Anglia, the squarish sash windows, and the shallow slated roof give this modest house the unmistakable hallmark of Suffolk.

LAXFIELD, SUFFOLK

An ancient mule track, skirting the churchyard, is flanked by a row of early-nineteenth-century brick cottages. The village has houses both of this beautiful orangey-pink brick and of the more conventional Suffolk colour of creamy white. The colour depends on the lime and iron content of the clay – more lime produces a paler brick. The relatively small pockets of different clays found in East Anglia provide these interesting contrasts. Laxfield was the scene of the martyrdom of John Noyes on 22 September 1557. Rather than accept Catholic doctrine, he elected to be burned at the stake. On the appointed morning all the villagers except one dowsed their fires. The one merely damped his down, so a wisp of smoke showed from his chimney. His fire was revived and used to fire the stake. A plaque recording this event is on the wall of the Baptist Chapel.

LAXFIELD, SUFFOLK

Weatherboarding is one of the cheapest building materials. It was frequently used for sheds and the rather more important outbuildings such as this small, two-storey structure that was probably used as a joiner's shop. The double doors on the first floor would allow long timbers to be hoisted up and the big windows would provide a good working light. It was once painted a creamy yellow, which has worn off to give a wonderful 'weathered' effect. Fortunately the aesthetic value of barns and farm buildings is now, just before it is too late, being appreciated, and many have preservation orders. One can only hope that very modest buildings like this one, originally made for a very different kind of village life, will also survive.

HOLME-NEXT-THE-SEA NORFOLK

The church of St Mary at Holme-next-the-Sea has an impressive flint tower in the Perpendicular style. The nave was rebuilt and the aisles removed in the late 1770s and it was at this time that the charming brick battlements were added to the tower. The village itself is rectilinear in plan. Behind the coast is a grid-like pattern of roads, possibly laid out by Roman surveyors to create a *colonia*. These roads formed boundaries to large land units, of 200 or 240 acres, which were subdivided in their turn. Ancient access to this district was provided by the Icknield Way, which ran from Avebury in Wiltshire. The parallel Peddar's Way was probably constructed after Boudicca's (Boadicea's) rebellion in AD 61. It was reserved for strictly military use and ends in the village.

GROOMBRIDGE, KENT

The Walks, so called, consists of a row of eighteenth-century cottages, placed behind pollarded limes and forming one side of the triangular village green. Here one can see nearly all the materials – red and blue brick, weatherboarding, hung tiles – that make Kentish vernacular architecture so charming. The village is part of the Groombridge Place estate. The house itself was rebuilt around the mid seventeenth century and has escaped all alteration and later 'improvement' beyond the installation of sash windows. The old house had the romantic distinction of being the prison of the Duke of Orleans, captured at the Battle of Agincourt by Henry V, in 1415.

GROOMBRIDGE, KENT

The village of Groombridge, in Kent, grew up around a private chapel, erected beside the road in 1625 by the owner of Groombridge Place, John Packer. It commemorates the outcome of an extraordinary incident in English history. King James I, seeking fresh European alliances, opened negotiations with Spain with a view to arranging a marriage between the future King Charles I, then Prince of Wales, and the Spanish Infanta. So fired with this idea was the young Prince that he set off incognito, in 1623, accompanied only by the Duke of Buckingham, to ride to Spain. Six months later they rode back again, their mission a complete failure. It was this failure that John Packer celebrated and he placed a tablet on the porch of his chapel to that effect!

CAWSTON, NORFOLK

North-eastern Norfolk has some of the most tortuous roads and lanes to be found in England. The land was enclosed for forest very early, leaving small, irregularly shaped fields. An old map of this village of Cawston shows that, by 1600, only ten per cent of the parish was open field. The rest of the land had either been enclosed between 1530 and 1580, or else was 'aunciently inclosed'. Cawston is noted in Domesday Book as having wood for 1,500 swine – only three other villages in the area had wood for more than 200. About a mile from the village, an urn on a pedestal, called the Duel Stone, commemorates a duel fought on Cawston Heath in 1698, when Oliver le Neve mortally wounded Sir Henry Hobart, whose family had built Blickling Hall. Cawston was a wool village and Cawston cloth was as renowned as worsted from the nearby village of Worstead.

GROOMBRIDGE, KENT

Groombridge is on a tributary of the Medway that forms the boundary between Kent and East Sussex. This group of cottages is on the road that leads down to the village green and presents a nice picture of various forms of seventeenth- and eighteenth-century cottage-building. The weather-tiling and tall chimneys are especially typical of the traditional Kentish style.

LONG MELFORD, SUFFOLK

Long Melford is on an ancient site. A Roman town lies under one end of the village and the main street is a slight diversion of the Roman road called Peddar's Way. The great village green, which runs the whole length of the High Street, is dominated on one side by the early Elizabethan mansion of Melford Hall and its handsome gateway, both built in the soft rose-red brick made in the village. The church is one of the most famous in England. It was expensively rebuilt in the late fifteenth century and still retains some magnificent medieval stained glass. Next to the church is Holy Trinity Hospital, founded in 1573 as almshouses for twelve poor men and two servants. The Regency front of the house on the left hides a much older, timber-framed building, while the row of five cottages further along the green is eighteenth century.

HEYDON, NORFOLK

Heydon is picturesquely clustered round a village green with the church on the north side. It is now rather larger than it was in the eighteenth century since it has absorbed two outlying hamlets, demolished in 1797 and 1838. This was to make way for the expansion of the park of Heydon Hall, a house built in the 1580s for Henry Dynne, an Auditor of the Exchequer, but altered and enlarged in the Victorian era. Heydon Hall is made of the very attractive local red brick, as is most of the village which is still 'family owned'. This unspoilt village has been used as a location for numerous films; it was the scene of the cricket match in the film of *The Go-Between*, made in 1970, starring Alan Bates and Julie Christie.

ORFORD, SUFFOLK

Orford, like so many Suffolk coastal villages, was once a flourishing sea port. Henry II built a large castle here in the twelfth century, which was to be a key fortress in East Anglia for the next 200 years. It remained more or less in its original condition until the 1600s. Now all that remains is the keep, a unique, irregular, eighteen-sided tower some ninety feet high. The best view of the pleasant brick and timber village is from the top of this tower. The keep has been in the care of a succession of private owners, among them the Marquesses of Hertford and Sir Richard Wallace, to whom we owe the Wallace Collection. Orford is now famous for its 'smokery', which smokes not only fish but a wide variety of other delicacies.

KERSEY, SUFFOLK

The village of Kersey has frequently been described as the most picturesque, and beautiful, of all the villages in south Suffolk. It consists of one long street of mostly pre-Reformation cottages, sweeping up to the parish church of St Mary. Instead of following along the river Brett, the village cuts directly across it. It is from this village that kersey cloth took its name, just as linsey-woolsey took its name from the neighbouring village of Lindsey. Kersey was a coarse cloth of twill weave, measured in 'pieces' originally sixteen to eighteen yards in length and less than a yard wide, but by the eighteenth century many kerseys were over forty yards in length. It was extremely good for keeping out the cold and wet and was exported to Europe in huge quantities, where it was made up into overcoats and army uniforms.

HOUGHTON, NORFOLK

Houghton was one of the first villages to be designed in the symmetrical Palladian manner. It was begun in 1729 – at the same time as the building of Houghton Hall – and was then referred to as the 'New Town'. It consists of two rows of five houses each, some almshouses and a couple of farmhouses, and lies just outside the beautiful south gates of the park of Houghton Hall. This spectacular house was built between 1727 and 1732 by Sir Robert Walpole when he was Britain's first Prime Minister. Designed by Colen Campbell, and with sumptuous interiors by William Kent, it was one of the first great Palladian 'palaces'. After years of neglect during the nineteenth century, it has now been restored to its former glory by the Dowager Marchioness of Cholmondely.

EDENSOR, DERBYSHIRE

The village of Edensor, in Derbyshire, was moved to its present position in 1839, because the sixth Duke of Devonshire preferred not to see it from his house, Chatsworth. The new village was laid out by Joseph Paxton, then the Duke's gardener, who was later to design the Crystal Palace, and the houses were designed by John Robertson. It is a monument to Victorian eclecticism as the houses have architectural features of every style: Italian windows, Tudor chimneys, Jacobean gables, Classical pediments, a Norman fountain by the green, Norman surrounds to the windows, half-timbering with brick infills and bargeboarding that could almost be Swiss. But Paxton's skilful layout manages to absorb all these conflicting features and the general impression is calm and uncontrived. The church dates from 1867 and was designed by Sir George Gilbert Scott.

LAVENHAM, SUFFOLK

Lavenham is one of the least changed of the Suffolk wool villages and it centres on one of the finest parish churches in England. Standing in the centre of the village, it is not difficult to imagine the scene when Queen Elizabeth I came here in 1578. She stayed at Long Melford with Sir William Cordell, who showed her round the county, accompanied by 200 young men in white velvet coats, 300 in black velvet and 1,500 retainers on horseback.

LAVENHAM, SUFFOLK

Here, at Lavenham, are some fifteenth- and sixteenth-century houses of the grander kind, the variation in treatment adding enormously to the charm of the whole picture. The exposed timbers of the 'black-and-white' house show the typical disposition of the uprights – rather close together with the occasional diagonal brace. The most interesting feature of this house is the way the first floor is jettied out on both sides, making full use of the corner position. The wall of the house on the left shows the timbers in their original condition, now weathered to a soft, silvery beige. The black painting of exposed timbers was nearly always done in the nineteenth century – perhaps to give what was considered a more 'olde worlde' effect.

SMARDEN, KENT

This higgledy-piggledy mixture of architectural styles and materials is typical of Wealden villages, being given a wonderful unity by the rich red tiling on the roofs. The entrance to Smarden churchyard is through the corner of one of these houses, which forms a sort of lych-gate; on the other side is a tiny quadrangle that is open to the street. The traditional 'Wealden house' had a central hall open to the roof, with service rooms at one side and the private living rooms at the other. The whole was set under one roof with the second storey always jettied out above the ground floor. These houses were built in great numbers in the late fifteenth and early sixteenth centuries.

SMARDEN, KENT

Smarden is a beautiful village of just one short street, with the church at one end. The uniform arrangement of white-painted brick with a weather-boarded superstructure is enlivened by the variety of window and door treatments.

SMARDEN, KENT

It was only in the fourteenth century that the forests of the Weald of Kent were cut down and permanent villages, such as Smarden, established. The church of St Michael was built at this time and remains unaltered. Its enormously wide nave and huge timber roof have earned it the nickname 'The Barn of Kent'. The forests were cleared to make way for sheep and, by 1333, King Edward III was seeking to encourage the wool trade by granting Smarden a charter to hold a weekly market and an annual fair. This charter, endorsed by Queen Elizabeth I, still hangs in the church. The excellent woollen broadcloth was taken by packhorse to the port of Faversham and there exported to the Continent. The prosperity brought by this wool trade is shown by the large number of fifteenth- and sixteenth-century houses in and around the village.

NETHER WORTON, OXFORDSHIRE

The church of St James in the remote north Oxfordshire village of Nether Worton, which lies in the valley of the river Tew, has a tower that is dated 1630. It is built of Cotswold stone, as is the tiny schoolhouse attached to the church. The unpretentious cottage, also of nicely mellowed Cotswold stone, is the schoolmaster's house. This small group of buildings that has survived over the centuries reminds us of the close connection that once existed between the Church and education.

BREAMORE, HAMPSHIRE

The regular squares of the timber framework, and the soft orange local brick, proclaim this row of cottages to be in Hampshire. The village of Breamore (pronounced Bremmer) is in two parts, one borders the main road, the other is romantically, and sparsely, disposed round a huge unenclosed common with a pond. This part of the village has a wonderful tranquillity. The church at Breamore is extremely ancient, begun by the Anglo-Saxons as long ago as AD 1000. Most unusually for that time it has a cruciform plan. There is an Anglo-Saxon inscription round one of the arches that means: 'Here the covenant is explained to thee'; and on the west wall there is the rather more recent admonition: 'Avoyd Fornication'.

BREAMORE, HAMPSHIRE

A pair of picture-postcard cottages, still unrestored and still with their old-fashioned, untidy gardens. They are at Breamore, in Hampshire; Breamore House, some distance from these cottages, was originally a very handsome late Elizabethan house, built in a beautiful red brick. It was burnt down, and largely rebuilt, in 1856. But perhaps the most interesting thing is to be found above the village, on Breamore Down. It is a maze, or 'mizmaze', cut through the turf into the chalk. There is a theory that medieval turf mazes had some inner symbolism, or penitential intent, but this one seems just to have been made for fun, the game being to get to the centre and out again, blindfold. Not easy to find, the mizmaze is 87 feet in diameter and has eleven concentric circles surrounded by yew trees. Turf mazes were more usually to be found on common land, nearer to the village.

PEMBRIDGE, HEREFORD AND WORCESTER

Pembridge is one of the prettiest villages in Herefordshire, centred round a small, triangular market place with an early-sixteenth-century market house. The ground stage is open, with eight carved posts, and there was originally an upper storey. The New Inn, which was new in the early seventeenth century, occupies one side of the market place. The village is built on a slope, down to the valley of the river Arrow, and as a result many of the streets have elevated, paved walks and the church, on an eminence, dominates the scene. This church of St Mary is basically of the fourteenth century and is remarkable for its bellhouse, which is separate from the main building. It is built mainly of wood and looks rather like a pagoda. Inside there is a most impressive timber structure housing bell and clock machinery.

WHERWELL, HAMPSHIRE

Wherwell (pronounced Werral) is in the Test valley and was the site of an important Benedictine Abbey, founded in AD 986 by Elfrida, widow of the Saxon king, Edgar. She spent the end of her life here as a penitent, in expiation of her part in the murders both of her first husband, Ethelwolf, and of her son, King Edward. During the thirteenth century, the redoubtable Abbess Euphemia ruled spiritually and practically. She diverted a streamlet of the Test to use for sanitary purposes, and this tiny stream now runs under the Priory, an early-nineteenth-century house standing on the site of the ancient abbey. These black-and-white timber-framed cottages look almost as if they have strayed from the Welsh borders. Only the heavy thatch, swept up over the windows, places them in this part of Hampshire.

LONGSTOCK, HAMPSHIRE

Longstock is a pretty Hampshire village on the river Test. This most famous of all trout streams flows from north to south through the western half of Hampshire, eventually flowing into Southampton Water. In the water meadows behind one of the farms are the remains of an old Danish dock known as 'the Moat', large enough to have accommodated the fearsome 'longboats' it is an extraordinary survival from the great Scandinavian invasions of England in the Dark Ages. Longstock is just one of the charming villages that lie on the banks of the river. They nearly all consist of rows of timber-framed cottages, sometimes with the red Hampshire brick exposed but more often colour-washed. The thatched roofs are generally swept up over tiny first-floor windows to give a 'raised eyebrow' effect.

LONGSTOCK, HAMPSHIRE

The only 'restoration' this old cottage at Longstock has received was in the early nineteenth century, when the stout little wooden-framed windows must have been inserted. The original timber frame is probably seventeenth-century and would have been filled with wattle and daub. As this rotted it was replaced by brick – perhaps at the same time as the change of windows – which was then rendered. The damp English climate, while encouraging lichen to grow on the thatch, is gradually wearing the plaster off the brickwork.

MORDIFORD, HEREFORD AND WORCESTER

This bridge over the river Lugg at Mordiford belonged, at one time, to the Hereford family. Its rent was a pair of golden spurs to be paid to the King of England whenever he rode across it. This was commuted, in 1304, to an annual payment of a pair of gilt spurs, to the value of six pennies, but by 1387 the rent had risen to three shillings and fourpence! A member of another well-known local family, Sir Barnabas Scudamore, successfully held Mordiford Bridge against the Scots in the seventeenth-century civil war. Until 1811, the church of the Holy Rood at Mordiford had, on its tower, a painting of a large green dragon, twelve feet long and with a red mouth and tongue. This was the famous Mordiford Dragon, which had lived in a wood nearby and was finally killed, after many attempts, by a condemned criminal.

SAPPERTON, GLOUCESTERSHIRE

Sapperton was the village chosen, in the early eighteenth century, by Lord Bathurst as his summer residence to 'escape the summer smells of Cirencester'. It was here that the two-mile-long canal tunnel linking the Thames and the Severn was opened by George III in 1789. When Ernest Gimson and the Barnsley brothers, followers of William Morris, came to Sapperton in the 1890s it had hardly changed – the cottages were still built entirely of local materials, and the work was all done by the men of the village. It was this atmosphere that appealed so strongly to Gimson. Believing in the gospel of healthy enjoyment for all in making useful and beautiful things, the three friends lived and worked in Sapperton for some twenty-five years. Their famous furniture workshop and showroom was housed in the oldest building in the village, Daneway House.

FRAMPTON-ON-SEVERN, GLOUCESTERSHIRE

Frampton-on-Severn lies on the flat land of the Vale of Berkeley. It is the perfect example of a village centred on a green – in this case, a very wide and long one with a huge variety of houses round it, nearly all of them set well back. As well as these houses from the seventeenth and eighteenth centuries, there is the very grand Frampton Court of the 1730s. In its garden there is 'a delicious Gothick bauble of a garden house', in the words of Sir Nikolaus Pevsner. The low line of green hills in the background is the beginning of the Forest of Dean, on the other side of the Severn.

LOWER SLAUGHTER, GLOUCESTERSHIRE

A tributary of the Windrush runs alongside the street in the Cotswold village of Lower Slaughter. It is crossed by many small bridges, some made of stone like this one, others of oak planks on stone pillars. The cottages are built of the traditional Cotswold material, stone, used for both walls and roofs. The stone tile quarries have been in use since at least Roman times, though the Romans preferred to shape their tiles with pointed ends. Many cottages in this part of the world were built on what was called the 'three-life system'. The landlord provided the site and the materials while the tenant provided the labour. The tenant, his son and grandson occupied it rent free and after that it reverted to the landlord. Some cottages were still lived in rent free under this system as late as 1912.

FILKINS, OXFORDSHIRE

Filkins is a handsome, compact stone village standing on the holiday route from Birmingham to Bournemouth. It was at one time nearly impassable during the summer months but, now bypassed, has achieved an almost transcendental calm. It was once the home of Sir Stafford Cripps, the post-war Chancellor of the Exchequer, who gave to the Parish Council a bowling green, a children's playground, a swimming pool, a surgery and facilities for hot baths. There is also a Carter Institute, given to the men of the village by a Miss Carter, on the firm understanding that no woman was ever to set foot in it. This ruling has since been suitably varied to accommodate the Women's Institute. Filkins has a most interesting local museum, a woollen mill, a gallery selling the work of local artists and craftsmen, and a church built between 1855 and 1857 by the architect G. E. Street.

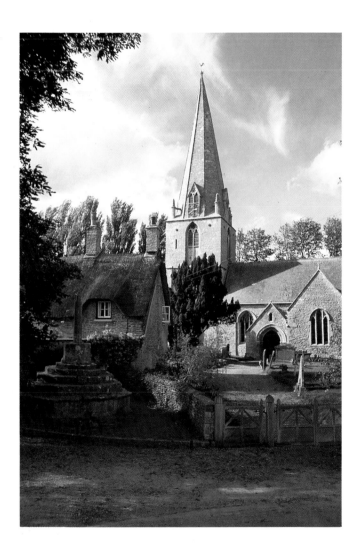

BROADWELL, OXFORDSHIRE

The church of St Peter and St Paul at Broadwell, in Oxfordshire, stands at the end of Dead Man's Lane, the road down which the corpses were carried from outlying parts of the parish for burial in the churchyard. The thatched house almost within this churchyard could well have been built originally as a parsonage. Under a handsome chestnut tree stands the shaft of a medieval cross, and the Old Manor, once the home of an almost forgotten novelist called Helen Ashton, stands opposite the church gate, overlooking the village green on its other side. Broadwell is divided only by a stream from its neighbour, Kencot. During the Second World War, the older men of both villages were employed in making an airfield about a mile away to which the wounded from the Normandy Beaches were flown for treatment in the hut hospital that had been built under the trees of Broadwell Grove.

EARDISLAND, HEREFORD AND WORCESTER

Eardisland is one of a trio of black-and-white villages in the valley of the river Arrow. Herefordshire is a county absolutely dominated by rivers and streams – in particular by the river Wye, which winds its way throughout the county – but, strangely enough, Eardisland is one of the very few villages actually on a river, possibly because this stream, unlike most of the others, is not subject to flooding. The Arrow is the stream that was crossed, between Pembridge and Eardisland, by Henry Tudor on his way to the Battle of Bosworth Field in 1485. He is supposed to have remarked: 'who would win a national strife must shoot the arrow first' – prophetic words, as it turned out.

EARDISLAND, HEREFORD AND WORCESTER

This unusually high brick dovecot was built in the seventeenth century to supply squabs (young pigeons) as winter fare to the Old Manor House of Eardisland. It has now fallen into disrepair, but adds greatly to the charm of the village. Across the road is the Old Schoolhouse – a black-and-white structure like most of the other buildings – which has been adapted for private use, although it still retains the old whipping post. Many of the houses scattered along the river stand on their original medieval croft. This was a piece of land owned exclusively by the householder and distinct from common fields and the village green. The result has been a most interesting variety in the siting of the houses.

WROXTON, OXFORDSHIRE

Wroxton, in north Oxfordshire, is a village built of tawny brown ironstone – marlstone – orginally quarried at Hornton. Most of the cottages are thatched and many were rebuilt after a fire of 1666. As in many English villages, the Post Office is simply a cottage with a posting box and porch added. Sanderson Miller, a local squire, amateur architect and pioneer of the mid-eighteenth-century Gothic Revival, helped to lay out the park of Wroxton Abbey. Sadly, most of his work for this ambitious scheme has disappeared; there was a lake with a great cascade and a circular temple. But his remodelling of the chapel at the Abbey and the tower of the parish church can still be seen. They were commissioned by Lord North in 1748. The Gothic Archway at nearby Drayton was part of the landscaping scheme for Wroxton and was probably also designed by Miller.

CROPREDY, OXFORDSHIRE

In this churchyard are buried some of the combatants from the Battle of Cropredy Bridge. Others lie in the trenches where they fell, in a field near the bridge, which was rebuilt in 1780. It was here that King Charles I, on 29 June 1644, defeated Waller, leader of the Cromwellian forces. One of the Roundhead leaders, Middleton, was taken prisoner and found himself dismounted among the King's forces. They mistook him for one of their own commanders, remounted him and wished him to make speed 'to kill a Roundhead'. By this means he escaped. Many relics of this battle were found during the nineteenth century and were housed in the village. Two suits of armour were hung up in the church, in perpetual memory.

SNOWSHILL, GLOUCESTERSHIRE

Snowshill is a small upland village in the Cotswolds, surrounded by open country once owned by the Abbey of St Mary at Winchcombe. It was this country that supported the vast flocks of sheep that made for prosperity in the fourteenth century. Dealers from all over Europe would regularly attend the great sheep shearings in the Cotswolds, although by the middle of the century the export trade was firmly held in English hands, in the shape of the Company of the Staple. English merchants made large fortunes from this wool trade and many Cotswold villages and small towns owe the beauty of their churches, and the magnificence of their houses, to them. The church of St Barnabas at Snowshill, however, was almost entirely rebuilt in a somewhat stolid fashion in 1864.

CASTLE COMBE, WILTSHIRE

Castle Combe, as its name implies, lies in a valley, or combe, in north Wiltshire, near the borders of Avon. The bridge crosses a fast-flowing stream that joins the river Avon at nearby Box. The old Cotswold stone houses and the magnificent church present an enchanting picture – it is no surprise that Castle Combe won the title of 'the prettiest village in England' in 1962. It is so unspoilt that it has been used extensively for film sets: it was, for example, the village in *Dr Doolittle*, made in 1967, starring Rex Harrison. Castle Combe belonged to the Scrope family for more than 500 years. A Scrope widow, Lady Millicent, married Sir John Fastolf, the original of Shakespeare's Falstaff. The now-forgotten G. Poulett Scrope, who lived here until 1867, was the author of a remarkable volume called *The Extinct Volcanoes of France*.

HALLATON, LEICESTERSHIRE

This seventeenth-century stone cottage has been pierced to allow access to a green lane. There are several of these lanes in the village, a relic of the days when Hallaton was a busy little market town. Although the cottage still retains its mullion and transom windows, the leaded lights on the ground floor have been replaced with larger panes. The alteration was probably made in the eighteenth or early nineteenth century when the dormer windows were added. The 'medieval' door is also a replacement.

HALLATON, LEICESTERSHIRE

Hallaton is one of the most attractive villages in Leicestershire; at its centre is the green, surrounded by pleasant houses and thatched cottages. On the green is the village cross in the form of a stepped circle with a conical roof. An ancient bequest required the rectors of Hallaton to provide two hare pies and two dozen penny loaves with ale, to be scrambled for on Easter Monday. Since 1771 the incumbents have been allowed to provide money rather than the actual pies, loaves and ale. However, the traditional game of choosing the Hallaton Bottle King still continues; it is played by kicking barrels and scrambling for hare pie.

BISLEY, GLOUCESTERSHIRE

Bisley, in the eighteenth century, had a large number of weavers working hand looms in their cottages. In 1733 these intrepid men successfully resisted the enclosure of the waste land where they kept their donkeys and pack horses. When, about a hundred years later, many commons in the area were enclosed a Lord Donington was standing for Parliament and as he drove about the countryside crowds would run beside his carriage shouting: 'Who stole the donkey's dinner!'

BISLEY, GLOUCESTERSHIRE

The spire of Bisley church is typical of the Gloucestershire style of the fourteenth century – narrow at the base and very slender. The church itself was built over the thirteenth and fourteenth centuries, but very extensively restored in 1862 in the neo-Romanesque style. In the churchyard is a Poor Soul's Light, which is thought to be the only one in England out of doors. It is a little hexagonal building in which candles were placed for masses to be said for the souls of the poor; it is built over a well and legend has it that it commemorates a priest who fell into the well and drowned as he was hurrying to a dying parishioner. Thomas Keble, brother of the more famous John – in whose memory Keble College, Oxford, was founded – was the rector of Bisley for nearly fifty years. Five water chutes, known as the Bisley Wells, were restored for Thomas Keble in 1863; they are at one end of the village and still discharge their pure water into great stone troughs.

CERNE ABBAS, DORSET

A Benedictine monastery was founded at Cerne Abbas in the late tenth century, but only the porch to the Abbot's Hall remains. There is also a magnificent fourteenth-century tithe barn. There was a boot-making industry here – Sir Walter Raleigh's boots, and the future Queen Victoria's first bootees, came from Cerne – and the excellent water produced excellent beer. Up to 1883, there were fourteen inns and alehouses in the village. A certain Alfred Thorne made hard hats here in the nineteenth century, 'so strong you could jump on them'. The Cerne Giant, north of the village, is a huge chalk figure cut into the turf. Thought to be a Romano-British representation of Hercules, he could also be an even more ancient fertility symbol, being well equipped for both roles. The village, ruinous and grass-grown in 1919, has now been splendidly restored.

STAPLEFORD, WILTSHIRE

The stone-built church of St Mary at Stapleford has spectacular Norman features, in particular the huge round piers of the south arcade. However, its exterior is mainly Decorated in style, a period of English church architecture that flourished from about 1290 to the middle of the fourteenth century. The church has a north tower – more usual in Wiltshire than in other counties – the top part of which is dated 1674. The little brick cottage next to the church has had its attached chimney stack refaced in rather unsympathetic cement. The small stack at the other end of the roof would have been similarly attached to an outside wall before the one-storey addition. This form of external chimney stack is a feature of thatch-roofed cottages, being designed to reduce the risk of fire.

PUDDLETOWN, DORSET

Puddletown is just one of a number of villages that owe their names to the river Piddle, or Trent, which meanders through Dorset to empty into Poole Harbour at Wareham. Piddletrenthide is certainly one of the more unlikely names, while Tolpuddle must be the most famous, being the birthplace of the Tolpuddle Martyrs – those brave Dorset men who, in 1834, were tried, convicted and transported for daring to ask for an average wage for their work. The near surroundings of Puddletown are especially interesting to archaeologists. Three-quarters of a mile away are the exceptionally well-preserved remains of Bardolfeston, a deserted village, and at Home Eweleaze can be seen Saxon strip fields superimposed on Celtic square ones. In addition, there are twenty-nine round barrows in the parish. Thomas Hardy, the great chronicler of Dorset, featured Puddletown as 'Weatherbury' in *Far From the Madding Crowd*.

EAST QUANTOXHEAD, SOMERSET

This archetypal village duckpond is at East Quantoxhead, on the edge of the Quantock Hills. Behind it is the church of St Mary and, just to be seen, the grey stone Jacobean house that has belonged to the Luttrell family since it was built. They bought their other house, nearby Dunster Castle, in 1376 but the land here has been in their possession since Magna Carta. In fact, it is reputed to be the only part of Somerset that has not changed hands since the Norman Conquest. The village is the background for the extraordinary story of Sarah Biffin. She was born into a village family here in 1784 without hands or arms. She early showed signs of artistic promise, drawing and painting by holding the pencil or brush in her mouth; she even became an expert needlewoman! She became something of a celebrity for her miniatures, was patronized by royalty and, in 1821, was awarded a medal by the Society of Artists.

MELBURY OSMOND, DORSET

Picture-book stone cottages with thatched roofs are set on a slope, down to the ford at Melbury Osmond. This is one of a group of villages and hamlets – Melbury Bubb, Melbury Abbas, East Melbury – of which the chief is Melbury Sampford. At Melbury Sampford is the remarkable Melbury House with its prospect tower built, in the early sixteenth century, by a Giles Strangways. The house was remodelled in the seventeenth century and again in the late nineteenth. It was a daughter of this house, Mrs Susanna Strangways Horner who, in 1745, built the nave of St Osmund's church at Melbury Osmund and gave a set of silver-gilt plate by Paul de Lamerie to the church. She died in 1758 and is buried at Melbury Sampford. The Oxford Clay, on which these villages lie, contains 'cement stone', which can be highly polished; it is then known as Melbury Marble.

LUCCOMBE, SOMERSET

Luccombe is a village of charming rustic cottages, mostly cream-washed with cosy thatched roofs; the perfect real-life versions of the Staffordshire pottery cottages that were made as pastille burners or money boxes. The vicar of Luccombe in the seventeenth century was Henry Byam, one of three ecclesiastical brothers holding livings in this part of the world. He was a staunch Royalist and lost four sons fighting for King Charles I – even his wife and daughter were drowned trying to escape to Wales. However, Henry Byam himself did escape and followed Prince Charles into exile. At the Restoration he returned to Luccombe and Selworthy of which he was also vicar and lived on until 1669. Both the church of St Mary here, and that of All Saints at Selworthy have large windows with elegant tracery of the same design, which is also used at nearby Cleeve Abbey.

POLPERRO, CORNWALL

The fishing village of Polperro would be hard to equal anywhere for quaint charm and it is a Mecca for artists as well as tourists. The village is hemmed in by steep hills on either side with small houses clinging to the slopes that lead down to the harbour, which is guarded at its entrance by jagged rocks – an entrance so narrow that it can be closed by a boom in rough weather. It was recorded as a fishing village early in the fourteenth century and the fishing industry continues today, if only in a small way. Polperro was the home of Dr Jonathon Couch who, as well as practising medicine and acting as advisor to his patients, was an antiquary and naturalist, publishing four volumes on the *History of the Fishes of the British Isles* in the 1860s. When he died his house became the museum it is today.

CLOVELLY, DEVON

Clovelly, on the coast of north Devon, is one of the show villages of England. Perched on the side of a hill, the steep and narrow main street is stepped and cobbled. Cars are barred from the village and wooden sleds are used for carrying loads and can be seen, as here, tied up outside the cottage doors. Many of the village houses are late Georgian in date and their sympathetic restoration and the unspoilt character of the village owes much to the work of Christine Hamlyn. She lived at Clovelly Court and carried out the work of restoration during the first twenty years of this century; her initials are on many of the whitewashed houses, both in the main street and the little, winding alleys that lead off it.

CLOVELLY, DEVON

Seen through a stone archway are the wooded cliffs that surround the village of Clovelly. Much of this woodland was planted by Sir James Hamlyn in the early nineteenth century. He also formed a three-mile-long drive to the east of the village, known as the Hobby Drive, which winds about the slopes. It was designed to give his friends and visitors a romantic view of the natural beauties of the countryside. From the cliff tops and, in particular from the area known as Mount Pleasant, now belonging to the National Trust, there are wonderful views of Lundy Island and across Bideford Bay.

CLOVELLY, DEVON

The miniature harbour at Clovelly has a curving pier and, beside it, a big old inn. Clovelly was just a small fishing village until Charles Kingsley made it famous in *Westward Ho!*, published in 1855. His father was rector of Clovelly from 1830 to 1836 and both Charles and his brother, Henry, spent their early years here. Henry Kingsley also wrote a stirring novel about Devonshire; it is his best-known book, *Ravenshoe*, published in 1862. Among the many monuments in the church, mostly to Carys but many to Hamlyns, the owners of Clovelly Court, Charles Kingsley is commemorated by a tablet.

BAMBURGH, NORTHUMBERLAND

Bamburgh Castle is in one of the most magnificent positions in England. It is placed on a steep outcrop of rock on the Northumberland coast and looks across the dunes and the sea to the Farne Islands. These islands are associated with nearby Holy Island as one of the cradles of Christianity in the north. It is here that St Aidan came for meditation. There is a legend that when he saw the pagan Penda of Mercia burning Bamburgh Castle he prayed mightily, the wind changed and the castle was saved. He died in Bamburgh in 651. By 1704, when it was bought by Lord Crewe, Bishop of Durham, Bamburgh Castle was in ruins. In 1757 a Dr Sharp made part of it habitable and installed a school, an infirmary and accommodation for shipwrecked sailors. In 1890 the castle was drastically restored and altered by Lord Armstrong.

BAMBURGH, NORTHUMBERLAND

Bamburgh is clustered round a green but the heart of the village is the great stone castle. The present building was started in the twelfth century but it has been much altered and restored. The Post Office is the house where the Victorian heroine, Grace Darling, died. The house in which she was born is opposite the church and next to it is the Grace Darling Museum. She was the daughter of the Longstone Lighthouse keeper in the Farne Islands. On 7 September 1838, the steamship *Forfarshire* was wrecked and Grace Darling and her father battled for many hours to save the survivors. The open rowing boat, only twenty-six feet long, in which they performed this deed is preserved in the museum.

WEST BURTON, NORTH YORKSHIRE

These nice, prosperous-looking houses at West Burton are set in some of the loveliest country in England. The village is at the meeting of Bishopdale and Walden Dale where Walden Beck flows down the valley to join the Ure in Wensleydale. Only a mile or two away are the famous Aysgarth Falls, three in number and one of the sights of Wensleydale. Wensleydale is renowned for its natural, unspoilt beauty and for the cheese of the same name. This cheese was originally made by the monks of Jervaulx Abbey from ewes' milk and the recipe was long kept a secret. Today it is made from cows' milk but still retains its high reputation and popularity.

HELTON, CUMBRIA

Helton lies on the easterly edge of the fells looking across the Eden valley to the great range of the Pennines. This row of cottages exemplifies the Cumbrian tradition of sober colouring, grey and white. The absolutely plain stone window and door surrounds are picked out with the contrasting colour, white on the cement-rendered cottages and grey on those that are whitewashed. On the common there is a druidical circle; a reminder of the length of time this rather inhospitable countryside has been inhabited and civilized. When the Romans invaded Gaul and, later, Britain, they found druidism to be the faith of the Celtic inhabitants. As well as religious belief this also embraced a judicial system, described by Caesar.

✦ THE VILLAGE HOUSE ✦

GREAT TEW, OXFORDSHIRE

Great Tew is on an ancient village site. Its Norman church has Saxon foundations. It is one of the few planned villages of the Tudor era and this range of early-seventeenth-century cottages reflects that time. It remains relatively untouched, the few alterations having been made very sensitively in the early nineteenth century. The principal tragedy must be the total destruction, by fire, of the beautiful Elizabethan house lived in by Lucius Cary, Lord Falkland – only the stables and the garden walls remain. A new house, 'Gothic' in feeling was built in the nineteenth century by Matthew Robinson Boulton, who purchased the whole estate in 1815. He was the son of Matthew Boulton, the famous Georgian ironmaster, who partnered James Watt in introducing steam power to industry.

If you were to travel from the Isle of Purbeck in Dorset towards the Wolds of Lincolnshire, you would pass through many villages made of stone: cream, grey, buff, tawny, almost orange, roofed with thatch or stone 'slates'. If, on the other hand, you were to start at Eastbourne and make towards Chester, you would find houses made of an astonishing variety of materials: stone, brick, exposed timbers and white plaster, or mixtures of all three, or perhaps weatherboarding and hung tiles, with roofs of tile and slate. In East Anglia you would find flints and brick, 'clay lump' and pantiles; on the borders of Wales, there is dark red sandstone used with black timbers and white-painted brick with roofs of huge stone slabs. Yet there is an underlying family likeness about all these houses, perhaps because so many village houses descend from two very ancient kinds of house, one that is now thought to have been known in Roman times, the other coming from the Saxons.

There is nothing Roman about the 'cruck-framed' house; merely, it is thought to have existed at that period. The Romans themselves used glass, brick and tiles in their villas and cities; not too much is known about the appearance of their isolated farmsteads and hamlets, though ground plans are now emerging from the silt fenlands of Bedfordshire. Perhaps the British who, in a manner of speaking, lived alongside the Romans, may have invented the cruck frame, or perhaps it came to this island with the Saxon mercenaries whom the Romans were obliged to hire in the fourth century AD, to protect them from other Saxons. We do not really know.

A cruck-framed house was built by splitting a tree and then placing the ends together to make an inverted V. This formed one end of the building and the same was done for the other. Then cross-beams were fixed across the inverted V's to convert them to A's, a ridge pole placed from point to point, and roof and wall timbers added as required. The spaces between the roof timbers were filled with woven hazel wands – wattles – and then thatched; wattles were also used between the wall timbers and 'daubed' with a mixture of mud and cow hair. This kind of house was built far into the Middle Ages and some still exist today.

The Saxon house, as reconstructed from excavations at West Stow in Suffolk, was made from split logs graduated to form a gable at each end of the house, with timbers of an equal height along the front and back and a door in one side, or at one end. There were no windows. Again the roof was thatched – with wheat straw or rye straw, or reed, or gorse, or bracken, or sometimes with heather or brushwood – and occupied about two-thirds of the height of the building. These houses had no foundations, or footings. The floor seems to have been sunken and would have been either of wood or beaten earth. When a house decayed beyond repair the occupants built again, perhaps at no very great distance from the previous site.

BARKWAY, HERTFORDSHIRE

This typical Hertfordshire village street is an excellent example of how cottages and houses of widely differing dates and styles can blend together to present a harmonious whole. The straightforward row of nineteenth-century flint and brick cottages sits happily beside its grand mid-eighteenth-century neighbour. This quite imposing village house would have been built for a prosperous lawyer or merchant. Further along, two charming bow windows have been inserted into a modest house to give a good view up and down the street. Barkway was a coaching village on the main road to Cambridge and it would have been full of the noise and bustle of horsedrawn traffic.

Whatever their provenance, these two house-types were the ancestors of the English village house. Whether converted into an L, or a T, or an H, or an E-shape, most village houses until well into the eighteenth century belonged to this family. Later, dormers were added in the roof, in some districts taking the form of gables at the front. The walls rose and the roof retreated. In the sixteenth century there were windows with tiny leaded panes of glass and the first floor extended over the ground floor to form a 'jetty', giving more room above, while keeping the lower walls dry and stabilizing the whole edifice. Chimneys appeared. The different local building materials offered a wonderful variety in the result, but they were variations on a theme. And, within the village, groups of houses in similar materials, of similar shape, but never quite identical, produced the harmony that is the hallmark of our more successful villages.

In terms of building history, these cottages, however picturesque and charming, represent a sharp retrogression from the time of the Romans. Our remote ancestors had lived in circular huts for upwards of four thousand years before the Romans came. These were made principally of timber – causing what is now recognized as an acute shortage of wood towards the end of the Iron Age – with conical roofs covered with hide, thatch, or turf. Over the four thousand years, the huts varied in size, from fifteen to forty-five feet in diameter. Some were made of stone and these have survived. On Dartmoor, isolated granite huts have been discovered, standing within large earth enclosures. In Dorset, a farmstead has been found, consisting of two circular huts side by side with a yard in front and paddocks to the north and south; there is evidence to suggest that this site was continuously occupied for three hundred years, though never by more than one family.

With the Romans all this appears to have ended. Their buildings were rectangular, their villas, made of brick and stone, roofed with tiles or possibly the local slate, were dry and centrally heated. Their mosaic floors have not been equalled in Britain since. Their farmsteads, regularly spaced, also had squared corners. When they left England, the Romans took their building skills with them, and so their buildings decayed. Unable to repair them, the remaining inhabitants abandoned them completely, and it was to be more than eight hundred years before brick reappeared in England.

If we may think of brick as mud that has been cooked, then uncooked mud has been used for building in districts short of stone for many centuries. The 'cob' of the West Country was a mixture of mud, gravel, pebbles and chopped straw, with lime to make it set. It was laid in layers about a foot thick, to make a wall that could be up to four feet wide. Each layer was trodden down and then left until it dried out before the next layer was laid. It was a slow process, depending rather on the weather. The outside was finished with colour wash – white, pink, cream and buff being the preferred colours, and a very deep layer of overhanging thatch was placed above it to keep it completely dry. Possibly our prehistoric ancestors used this method, too, but as cob melts in the rain, all traces would have disappeared.

The 'clay lump' of East Anglia was not quite the same. For this the clay was moistened, covered with chopped straw, and trodden down by horses. It was then placed in wooden moulds and left to dry out, giving a slightly crisper effect than cob, which tends to look as though it has been poured.

Where flints were plentiful in clay areas, they were introduced into the cob or clay, and gradually took over from it. Flints require a great deal of mortar and are very awkward when it comes to corners. Many church towers made with flints are round for this reason. Cob, clay and flint, together with wood used in various ways, were the building materials used in districts where stone was rare or non-existent, before the re-introduction of brick.

Bricks appeared again in the late twelfth century in Essex and Suffolk, both made locally and imported from Flanders; it was the Flemings who established brick-making in East Anglia. There are two principal ways of laying bricks: English Bond, which consists of a course of bricks laid lengthways – stretchers – followed by a course of bricks laid endways – headers, and Flemish Bond, in which headers and

WHALTON, NORTHUMBERLAND

The houses and cottages at Whalton nearly all have big front gardens giving on to the grassy verge of the main street. This cottage is no exception. Just beyond it is the Manor House. This was originally four, much altered village houses which, in 1908, were converted into one house by Sir Edwin Lutyens. The strange juxtaposition of the corbelled bow windows with the very plain main façade has been most skilfully handled and the effect is one of great charm and unity.

stretchers are laid alternately in the same course. A third method, called 'nogging', where bricks are laid obliquely in alternate rows, is used to fill in the spaces between timbers. Different-coloured bricks, blue, brown and red, cream and yellow, occur locally all over England. They were originally quite small, their width convenient to the hand, but a tax was put on bricks in 1784, after which they grew a bit thicker. They have been a standard size, and made by machine, since the 1880s.

So bricks came to be used at the corners of flint houses and as the chimneys of cob houses. They were combined with 'clunch', large blocks of solid chalk; they were left exposed, or painted, or covered with roughcast. Versatile, decorative and practical, they gave a permanence to many small houses made of less durable materials and helped to preserve them.

The limestones of England are some of the most beautiful building stones in the world, from Portland stone, which is almost white when new, through the silver-grey of Purbeck, to the golds of Bath and the Cotswolds and the greys of Northamptonshire, Barnack and Ketton, with their underlying buffs and pinks. They are easy to handle, being hard but not too hard, and there is a certain lightness about the buildings they produce.

Heavier stones make more solid, frequently rather lower buildings. The granite and gritstone of the south-west, the strongly coloured sandstones of the Welsh borders, the grey limestones and buff sandstones of the Pennines, the hard chalk of the Yorkshire Wolds, the Coral Rag of the Vale of White Horse, the Kentish Rag of the Weald, have all produced styles exactly suited to the material. And perhaps that is the secret of English village-building. The material is never asked to do what it does not want to do, never forced into a preconceived pattern. A rural building tradition is slow to ripen and slow to change, an inner process. Village houses are made from local materials, adapted to local conditions, and signs of outside influence are rare.

The traditional roofs of England are as interesting as the walls. Thatch was the original covering, to be replaced by tiles in the clay lowlands, made in the Midlands from the fifteenth century. Like the clay, they come in all colours, reds and browns, and almost orange. In the Weald tiles were also hung on walls, called 'weather-tiling', frequently combined with 'weatherboarding', which consists of overlapping painted wooden planks. Pantiles – tiles with an interesting S-bend – are thought to have come from Holland in the seventeenth century and to have been made in England since the eighteenth. They were found mostly in East Anglia, the Fens, and in the south-west.

In areas where there is stone, the houses have stone roofs, pitched very high on the solid houses of the Cotswolds, rather lower in the north and on the borders of Wales. A roof of stone slabs weighs perhaps five times as much as one of slate or tile. There are stone 'slates' in Northamptonshire, Oxfordshire, Devonshire and the Pennines, and Horsham slabs in Sussex; truer slates come from the Lake District – where they are grey-blue to almost olive in colour – the Forest of Dean and Swithland, in Leicestershire. The dark-grey slate that is more or less universal today was brought from Wales by the railways.

It is the blending that satisfies, of local brick with local tile, local stone with local slate, whitewash with thatch, buildings produced from the ground on which they stand, part of it. It would, however, be foolish to pretend that many of these charming dwellings were not, until the present day, scenes of the acutest discomfort. When they were built they were damp, difficult to heat and almost impossible to keep clean. There are many villages still not reached by the main sewer. Bathrooms were not considered essential in cottage buildings until after the Second World War, and many country people now in their fifties grew up without the convenience of electricity.

It is now possible to combine the romance of the past with the practical advantages of the present. Until about 1850, if one had been transported blindfold into an English village, one would have had some idea of one's whereabouts. Since then standardization has set in. Building in villages is no longer the art it was; local materials, local styles, local shapes are all ignored. Usually it is the proportion that particularly displeases, building regulations now insist that rooms should be at least 7 feet 6 inches or 8 feet high, which has the effect of making small houses look top heavy. But doing up tumbledown cottages – 'gentrification' as it is now most unfortunately called – is an even more dangerous art, the aim in so many cases being simply to raise the social status of the building. Village houses in general have an integrity, an innate honesty and self-sufficiency that would need neither apology nor excuse in any society less class-ridden than ours. The guinea stamp of carriage lamp, wrought-iron gate and swinging flower basket is quite superfluous. Like many of their previous occupants, these houses have a character to preserve; and one ignores that at one's peril.

PEWSEY, WILTSHIRE

Cruck construction is one of the oldest methods of building used in England. As can be seen here, it consists of finding two inclined, or sometimes 'knee-ed', timbers, placing them tip to tip and then tying them in with horizontal beams. Sometimes one great tree was split in two to obtain exactly matching timbers. The resulting rough triangle was then filled in with wattle and daub, or sometimes brick. Generally the timbers were concealed by rendering, but when exposed and painted – as in this example at Pewsey – they form a pleasing pattern. This sort of black-and-white architecture is comparatively rare in Wiltshire, being more often associated with the Welsh border country, where whole villages of this type can be found.

PEWSEY, WILTSHIRE

Pewsey is on the river Avon, in Wiltshire, and gives its name to the vale that separates the Marlborough Downs from Salisbury Plain. The Kennet and Avon Canal also passes by Pewsey, and on through the Vale of Pewsey on its way to Bath. About a mile away is the famous White Horse that was cut into the turf in 1785, and re-cut in 1937 to commemorate the Coronation of George VI. It is one of seven White Horses that were cut in Wiltshire during the eighteenth and early nineteenth centuries.

COCKFIELD, SUFFOLK

The tiny windows of this typical East Anglian cottage are designed to keep out the freezing winds that sweep across the flat countryside, and the thick cob walls and thatched roof ensure a snug interior. The exterior chimney stack reduced the risk of fire. The cottage is at Cockfield and is in the process of being re-thatched. Thatch, the oldest kind of roofing, can be of reed or straw, both now in short supply; indeed, a special kind of wheat must now be grown to give long straw for thatching. Cockfield is one of the largest villages in west Suffolk and consists of 'nine registered greens' and various hamlets. Its station was on the Great Eastern Railway between Bury St Edmunds and Long Melford and, when it was opened in 1872, all the schoolchildren were given a day's holiday to watch the first train come through.

MONKS ELEIGH, SUFFOLK

A 'hall house' of a particularly Suffolk kind, so called because the hall, or main room, of the house was placed at one end of the long side, with parlour, kitchen and pantry close to it. This type of house was the most usual pattern throughout the sixteenth and seventeenth centuries in the English countryside. This one has had an addition tacked on with a thatched roof and detached chimney stack. The L-shape is to be seen in nearly all Suffolk farmhouses of this date and provides some degree of protection from the biting east winds. Monks Eleigh is a compact, neat village of the sort that would have been perfectly self-sufficient in the eighteenth century. Suffolk has only one city and not many towns. It was on the larger villages such as this that the outlying, smaller villages and hamlets relied for their goods and trade.

ROLVENDEN, KENT

Traditional white weatherboarding on a brick base has been used for these houses at Rolvenden, in Kent, a village fortunate enough to have a Post Office, a stationer and a baker. The main village street, ending in the church, is lined on each side with houses like these. In the 1890s, Frances Hodgson Burnett, famous as the author of *Little Lord Fauntleroy*, came here and rented 'the big house', Great Maytham Hall. She is thought to have based the wilderness in *The Secret Garden* on the high-walled garden of that house. In 1909, it was rebuilt and enlarged by Sir Edwin Lutyens in the neo-Georgian style.

ROLVENDEN, KENT

A perfect example of the wonderfully neat detailing that is typical of Kentish weatherboarded houses. This cottage at Rolvenden would have been built by a local builder and it is interesting to see, for example, how carefully the flashing has been placed over the windows. The very restrained use of black and white paint adds to the 'doll's house' effect. Indeed, it is really only the martins' nests under the eaves that make one realize that this is a full-sized house!

PEASENHALL, SUFFOLK

A row of pleasant, if undistinguished, cottages at Peasenhall has been given life and character by the uninhibited use of strong colour. This is unusual in an English village, where there is a tendency to conform even when the authority of a common landlord is lacking. This village was the scene of a sensational murder case in 1902, resulting in the unusual verdict of 'not proven' despite the fact that the defendant, William Gardiner, was considered definitely guilty by the majority of the inhabitants! Peasenhall has the distinction, now rare, of a village shop – Emmetts – which has been run by the same family for three generations. They also hold the Royal Warrant for ham, pickled according to their secret recipe.

THAXTED, ESSEX

Almshouses can often provide a key to village history and a fascinating insight into what our ancestors considered to be adequate living accommodation. An enormous number still exist all over the country in villages and small towns. Fortunately, the Victorians as well as endowing a great number of charitable institutions themselves, looked to the repair and maintenance of many earlier almshouses. Their efforts in this respect – aesthetically speaking anyway – were nearly always more fortunate than those expended on our parish churches. This pretty row of almshouses at Thaxted in Essex is decorated with 'ginger bread' barge-boarding and, although based on the typical one-room-cottage plan, has had dormer windows introduced into the roof spaces; the matching row directly behind has thatch roofs.

UPPER SLAUGHTER, GLOUCESTERSHIRE

Upper Slaughter has attracted the attention of several eminent architects, including Sir Edwin Lutyens, the designer of New Delhi, and Sir Guy Dawber, architect of a number of delightful neo-Georgian country houses. They both worked here between 1906 and 1910, remodelling existing buildings as well as designing new houses. All the houses in the village are of stone from the many old quarries in the parish and most have Cotswold stone roofs. Before the advent of the motor car in the 1920s, these Cotswold villages were very difficult to get to and they relied entirely on local materials for building. The sense of unity, and the use of age-old village crafts that produced the village of Upper Slaughter, appealed very strongly to followers of the Arts and Crafts Movement of the 1880s, and those who advocated a return to the crafts-manship of the Middle Ages.

GREAT TEW, OXFORDSHIRE

This row of picturesque cottages is on the northern green in the village of Great Tew. The beautiful planting of evergreens throughout the village, and the neatly clipped box hedges in front of the cottages, are monuments to the taste of John Claudius Loudon. This young Scotsman came to Great Tew when he was only twenty-six and was put in charge of some 1,500 acres of the estate owned, at the time, by Colonel Stratton. Here Loudon ran a sort of agricultural school for the sons of landed proprietors and farm bailiffs, and in 1807 published an account of the results obtained. Meanwhile, he kept on his landscape gardening practice, making 'improvements' to the village that have greatly added to its present appearance.

GREAT TEW, OXFORDSHIRE

The perfect English cottage, its picturesqueness sadly caused by ruin and decay. There have been problems of late in the village of Great Tew, some of which has achieved an advanced state of dilapidation. This village is one of the most interesting in the whole of Oxfordshire and has always been in private hands. Early in the nineteenth century, when it was still the fashion to sweep away or, at best, to move whole villages, this one was fortunate enough to engage the attention of John Claudius Loudon, who strongly disapproved of such ideas.

GREAT TEW, OXFORDSHIRE

Great Tew was once the home of Lucius Cary, Lord Falkland, after whom the village inn, the Falkland Arms, is named. He and his wife Lettice came to live here after their marriage in the early 1630s. Here he kept open house for writers and scholars such as Abraham Cowley, Edmund Waller and Ben Jonson who, in the words of Lord Clarendon, 'frequently resorted and dwelt with him as in a College situated in a purer air'. Lucius was killed at the Battle of Newbury in September 1643. To quote Lord Clarendon again: 'if there was no other brand upon this odious and accursed Civil War than that single loss, it must be most infamous and execrable to all posterity'. Of his house nothing remains; but the ghost of his grandfather, from whom he inherited, is said to drive in a coach and six round a great elm tree in the park.

DUNSTON, NORFOLK

This handsome weather-boarded mill, with its adjacent miller's house, has now been turned into a restaurant, typical of the excellent attitude that prevails towards conservation in the county. It lies just south of Norwich, on the river Tas. The whole of Norfolk is scattered with mills of various kinds, both wind and water, used originally for grinding grain but now converted, many of them, into private houses or, as here, restaurants. Dunston is one of several villages in the Tas valley that lie between Tasburgh and Norwich. At the time Domesday Book was compiled this was one of the most densely populated areas, with many very small parishes. Norwich itself, at the end of the seventeenth century, was the second largest city in England.

DOWNTON, WILTSHIRE

An old mill house on the river at Downton, on the borders of Hampshire and Wiltshire. Wiltshire has a number of 'new towns' from the early thirteenth century, of which Salisbury, with its main grid of streets dating from 1220, must be the most important. But Downton also has a thirteenth-century new town called The Borough, across the Avon from the old village. It was created by Peter des Roches, Bishop of Winchester, and consists of two long rows of houses with a broad strip of grass between, the plan of several villages in the extreme north of England built after the 'harrying of the north' in 1069. Downton returned its own Member of Parliament in the seventeenth century. One of them, Sir Charles Duncombe, Receiver of Customs under Charles II and James II, much displeased the latter by 'refusing £1500 to carry him over sea'. He died the richest commoner in England and is buried in Downton Church.

GREAT BEDWYN, WILTSHIRE

This amazingly decorated cottage belongs to Mr Lloyd, the stonemason at Great Bedwyn, and acts as an enchanting advertisement for the art. This village lies on the edge of Savernake Forest, west of Hungerford and just over the border into Wiltshire. In the past, communication was by the Kennet and Avon Canal, begun in 1786 to connect Newbury with Bath. Nowadays, Great Bedwyn boasts one of the few village railway stations on a main line that is still in operation. Fast trains to London make this a favourite spot for commuters to settle, or have weekend cottages. The village itself suffered a disastrous fire in the nineteenth century, after which much of it was rebuilt in the style of Mr Lloyd's house.

TURNASTONE, HEREFORD AND WORCESTER

You would have to travel far to find a more perfectly preserved example of a village garage than this one. In the years when the horse was being replaced by the motor car, and the village blacksmith was turning into a garage mechanic, the village forge was transformed into a garage. The lovingly kept Raleigh bicycle advertisement – almost life size – that graces the front wall is a memorial to the hugely popular summer sport of 'cycling' that reached its height in the 1930s. Matching green petrol pumps are as immaculately kept as the yew arch that frames the door. Turnastone is divided from the village of Vowchurch by the river Dore. The two churches are reputed to have been built by two quarrelling sisters, one of whom said to the other: 'I vow I will build my church before you turn a stone of yours.'

BOSSINGTON, SOMERSET

Bossington lies on the hills, right on the edge of Exmoor, overlooking Porlock and Porlock Bay in west Somerset. It has plenty of pretty cottages, some built of the local, reddish stone with tile roofs and some of either stone or cob and whitewashed, with thick thatched roofs. Despite the sprinkling of snow, the climate is mild enough to have allowed this unusual treatment of a variegated evergreen, which has grown tall and been trained against the cottage walls. Bossington is one of a group of villages that seem quite remote and cut off, bounded on the north by the sea and on the south by the main A39 road between Minehead and Lynton.

CADGWITH COVE, CORNWALL

Snug cottages at Cadgwith Cove on the Lizard Peninsula in Cornwall. The whitewashed walls are typical of Cornish fishing villages and the blue painting of the door and window frames is also traditional; the thatched roofs are the common alternative to the more usual slate. The whole of the south coast of Cornwall with its many tiny bays and inlets and general inaccessibility is well suited to smuggling, which, together with wrecking (the carrying off of goods from wrecked ships), formed a considerable part of the livelihood of the inhabitants. So much so, indeed, that when, in the seventeenth century, Sir John Killigrew proposed to build a lighthouse at the Lizard, there was a fearful outcry in the neighbourhood and it was not until 1751 that a lighthouse was built. Today, Cadgwith boasts a coastguard and a lifeboat station.

EAST COKER, SOMERSET

The Helyar almshouses were founded in 1640 by Archdeacon Helyar, the owner of Coker Court. The Archdeacon had been Chaplain to Queen Elizabeth I and had married one of her cousins. He bought Coker Court from the Phelips family who had lived there during the building of Montacute House, which then became their home. East Coker is a handsome village, built almost entirely of the local Ham Hill stone. It is particularly unspoilt and descendants of many of the families named in the old Parish Register of 1560 still live in the village. 'Eliot' is one of these names. The poet T.S.Eliot came back to the home of his forefathers and his ashes are buried in the church.

ALLERFORD, SOMERSET

This picturesque packhorse bridge at Allerford was built in the days when there was no other form of transport than the horse. Throughout this hilly country packhorses and mules were used to carry goods from one remote little village to another, in particular raw wool and finished cloth. Where no carts could go, laden animals carried the wool to the spinners and weavers in outlying villages and collected the cloth. This was the industry that brought such prosperity to the west of England during the Middle Ages. The attractive brick and stone cottage on the banks of the stream has a round bread oven built out of a side wall and a great tall chimney.

TINTAGEL, CORNWALL

The most famous of all Cornish stone cottages is the Old Post Office in Tintagel. In reality it is a rare survival of a small manor house built in the fourteenth century. However, Tintagel's main claim to fame must rest with the legend of King Arthur. The romantic remains of Tintagel Castle on the headland or Island have inspired writers and poets throughout the centuries since Geoffrey of Monmouth who, in the twelfth century, wrote of it as the birthplace of King Arthur, to Tennyson and *The Idylls of the King*, 1859. It was in Merlin's Cave, on the beach at Tintagel, that Tennyson placed the meeting between Arthur and Merlin. Geoffrey of Monmouth's *History of the Kings of Britain* spread the fame of Tintagel throughout Europe; other English writers associated with it include Malory, Spencer, Matthew Arnold and even Swinburne who came here to finish *Atalanta in Calydon*.

TEFFONT MAGNA, WILTSHIRE

This large village house was in fact built in 1700, although still in the style of the mid seventeenth century, with its mullioned windows and steep gables. This shows how long it took for new architectural fashions to penetrate the deep countryside from London. The house is to be found in the pleasant, tranquil village of Teffont Magna on the banks of the river Nadder. The village has an ancient church, parts of which are thought to date from the ninth century. The immediate district is remarkable for the elaborate names of its villages – Teffont Evias, Fisherton Delamere and Fonthill Gifford, for instance. The latter was the village of the ill-fated Fonthill Abbey, an extravagant folly of the very late eighteenth century, whose central tower, 225 feet high and built on wholly inadequate foundations, finally collapsed in 1825.

VERYAN, CORNWALL

The two round houses guard the entrance to the village of Veryan on the neck of the Roseland peninsula; undoubtedly one of the most beautiful parts of Cornwall. The evocative name of Roseland signifies heath or promontory land. These Regency Gothic follies are but two out of five similar cottages in the village – they were reputedly built by a vicar of Veryan to house his five spinster daughters and are round in shape to avoid any corners for the devil to hide in! The pretty church in its leafy setting is named St Symphorian, just one of the many unusual saints' names much in evidence throughout Cornwall, a reminder of its Celtic past. Towards the coast but still in the parish of Veryan is one of the largest round barrows in Britain.

ODSTOCK, WILTSHIRE

This house was the parsonage farmhouse and was built on glebe land. Glebe land was originally allocated for the support of the parson and could either be farmed by him, or let for farming or, from the nineteenth century, for building – or even mining! However, the ancient parsonage house itself, and the ten acres most convenient to it, could not be leased and the proceeds of this land were the absolute property of the parson. Odstock, where this house is situated, originally had a Norman church, remodelled in the thirteenth century and rebuilt in 1870; so the glebe lands have an ancient history. Glebe House is seventeenth-century – the widely spaced windows and short wings are unusual; and the 'mushrooms' on either side of the front door are old staddle stones.

CONSTANTINE, CORNWALL

The village of Constantine is named after its church. St Constantine is a rather grand edifice built of large, regular granite blocks provided by the quarries in the north of the parish – the tall west tower commands views of the surrounding countryside. This Cornish village is situated on a hill between two streams that feed the Helston river and the large, wooded inlet where the river meets the sea. Stone walls and slate roofs are the rule in Cornwall, making full use of the natural materials of the country. These rather austere cottages are given a hint of style by the charming arrangement of glazing bars in the sash windows – a typical pattern of the early nineteenth century.

TREGATTA, CORNWALL

Stone cottages in the tiny community of Tregatta in north Cornwall on the road between Tintagel and Camelford. The sturdy stone porches with their slated roofs are typical and have been built to keep out some of the fierce wind that seems to blow continually on this coast. The prefix 'Tre' is used extensively and indiscriminately throughout Cornwall; hardly surprising as the meaning is in old Cornish 'a farm' and, latterly, 'a town'. The whole of this part of the country is closely associated with the Arthurian legend – nearby is Slaughterbridge where his last battle was fought and his supposed burial place is at Warbstow Bury, while Dozmary Pool on Bodmin is the setting for the appearance of the great sword, Excalibur. Tregatta itself is only about a mile from Tintagel, the centre of the Arthurian myth.

CLAPHAM, NORTH YORKSHIRE

A tiny triangle of green marks the meeting place of the track over the bridge and the village street in the small village of Clapham. At the time it was built it was in the West Riding of Yorkshire, quite close to the Westmorland border. The greyish-brown cement finish used on most of the houses is reminiscent of the Lake District. These large cottages are basically of the eighteenth century, but the smallest one has been 'Gothicized' by the addition of Victorian Gothic windows. The grey local stone has been used, not only for the bridge but also for the garden walls, adding much to the atmosphere of this moorland village.

DENT, CUMBRIA

The remote village of Dent is on the western side of the Pennines in what was once the West Riding of Yorkshire but is now the new county of Cumbria. It is the only village in the Dent valley, which leads to the beautiful little town of Sedbergh, some six miles away. Like most of the hill villages in this part of the world the houses are huddled together, as if for warmth. They are mostly built of local stone and generously cream- or whitewashed, with grey slate roofs. An austere colour scheme that admirably suits the atmosphere of the great, bare hillsides and sharp northern air.

ASKHAM, CUMBRIA

A little country road leads from Penrith to the village of Askham. One's expectations are raised by the exciting view of Lowther Castle just before one enters the village. In fact, this is less dramatic although charming in its way. A broad, tree-lined street leads down to Askham Hall, the house of the Earl of Lonsdale, a descendant of the builder of Lowther Castle. The Lowther family have been the great land and political magnates in, what is now called, Cumbria for generations. Indeed, James Lowther, Earl of Lonsdale who died in 1802, controlled nine seats in Parliament; they were known as 'Jemmy Lowther's ninepins'. Lowther Castle was built between 1806 and 1811 to the design of Robert Smirke. He was only twenty-five and had just returned from a tour of Greece. Despite this, Lowther Castle is in the Picturesque Gothic style. Sadly, it is now a ruin and the roof was taken off in 1957.

ASKHAM, CUMBRIA

One of many village houses at Askham in Cumbria that bear a date. This one, of 1674, shows a surprisingly sophisticated door frame with its upward curving ears. The brilliant, deep red is a typical colour of this part of the world and does much to enliven the grey stone or, as in this case, cement-faced cottages. The village itself belongs more, in style, to the North Riding of Yorkshire with cottages running down each side of a broad, tree- and grass-lined street.

WHALTON, NORTHUMBERLAND

One-storey cottages in the village of Whalton in Northumberland. It is an interesting fact that the further north you go, in England, the more these one-storey houses are to be found – that is, discounting the ubiquitous twentieth-century bungalow. By the time Scotland is reached whole villages of one-storey cottages are discovered, giving a very French and somewhat dour appearance.

WHALTON, NORTHUMBERLAND

Whalton is a village strung out along a main street. The very attractive houses and cottages are all set well back behind wide, tree-set, grass verges. The rather prim look is due to it being an 'estate' village and nearly all built of the local, golden brown stone, with the added uniformity of white-painted doors and window frames. On 4 July the old custom of marking Midsummer's Eve is celebrated by dancing round a bonfire, still called Baal-fire from its pagan origins.

✦ VILLAGES IN THE LANDSCAPE ✦

SOUTH NEWTON, WILTSHIRE

South Newton lies on the river Wylye, which rises near Stourhead and flows to Wilton to be joined by the Nadder. The high land between these two rivers is covered by Groveley Wood. At the neighbouring village of Great Wishford, Oak Apple Day – celebrating the escape of Charles II after the Battle of Worcester, when he hid in an oak tree – is ushered in to cries of 'Groveley! Groveley! Groveley! and all Groveley!' It was through South Newton that the suitors for common rights of pasture would go, on Whit Tuesday, from Great Wishford to the Cathedral of Salisbury 'in a dance', carrying boughs to lay on the altar, at the same time paying their dues, Pentecostals or Smoke-Farthings.

Wherever you go in England, over closely cropped, bare-backed downs, through deep lanes, across high moors, over brilliant green meadows with white foaming hedges, through flat cornfields and reed-bordered backwaters, across desolate heathland or down tree-filled valleys, someone has been there before you.

Thousands of years ago – and the latest estimate seems to be twelve – when man first came to these islands, they were covered by a dense forest, of beech and hornbeam, oak, ash and elm, with silver willows and trembling poplars in the marshlands and river beds, alders and rowans and birches. And man began to cut them down.

Those trees were not replaced. The wild moorland on the hilltops, so loved by Lorna Doone and Catherine Earnshaw, glowing with heather and gorse and now deep in masses of bracken, were created then. The blanket bog, the peat hags, the lonely tarns and pools with their marshy edges, where the rush-grass and the bog-cotton, and perhaps the marsh orchis, grow, come from that time. The chalk downlands were stripped bare and began, very slowly, to leach into the valleys so that they are now thought to be at least three feet lower than they were.

They had excellent axes, those distant ancestors, of flint or very hard rock, made in 'factories' as remote from one another as Cornwall and the Lake District. Trackways formed at that time have recently been found in Somerset, so we may suppose a network of trading routes all over England. No doubt, the hilltops once cleared, stayed so, as it is not easy to persuade trees to grow on chalk downland or windswept heathland.

Some of their village sites are known to us, nearly all in places difficult of access, bleak and desolate, now abandoned to the sheep and heather. Other villages, more sheltered and congenial, have long since disappeared beneath the plough; but the fact that people *also lived* in what are now wild, inhospitable places, suggests a large population indeed, living in an intensely cultivated landscape. Some drainage they certainly did; no doubt many a small stream still wending its way towards the brimming river was invented, or at least assisted on its journey, by our Neolithic forebears.

They lived in villages and dug pits to store their grain, using them later for their rubbish. At a site in Suffolk, recently excavated, two hundred pits were found, indicating a very large settlement. It was they who made the huge stone circles at Avebury and Stonehenge and who buried their dead in the long barrows and regular mounds that give much of Wiltshire an artificial look; and they continued to cut down the trees.

Their fields were small and square, separated by banks or ditches; the plants that needed greater attention, flax, hemp and saffron, grown near their houses, wheat and barley further away. They used the two-course system, growing a crop one year and letting the field lie fallow the next. By the beginning of the Bronze Age, 3,500 years ago, the population was large enough for territories to be marked out. Aerial photography shows banks and ditches in the west of England running for several miles, enclosing huge areas of what is now downland, sometimes with focal points from which the boundaries radiate. Smaller areas were marked out at this time, too, divisions of land that could well have been the foundation of our field system. On the Yorkshire moors, territorial markings have been discovered from this time, though these may only have been summer grazing areas.

All the indications are of a crowded, almost over-populated country. In the first century BC it is probable that there were fewer trees than there are now and that the divisions of land had developed into estates, fiercely defended and intensely cultivated.

This was the landscape that the Romans found. It was not a dense forest through which our ancestors, painted blue, swung from branch to branch. Julius Caesar, in 55 BC, referred to the huge population, the enormous flocks, the farms and homesteads 'all over the place'. The people inland did not grow corn, he said, neither did the beech or the pine grow there. Possibly, making his way across Kent towards Middlesex, he travelled over soil that was too heavy for the ploughs of those days; but there can be no doubt that the beeches and pines – native trees both and still much in use for building and furniture – were not there because they had already been cut down.

The Romans placed their farmsteads and settlements at very regular intervals, as we may now find from recent discoveries in Bedfordshire. They dug wells and settled the high chalklands; they continued to drain the marshes. When they left England in the fifth century AD, it is conjectured that they left behind a population of nearly five million people. When it was next measured, by the Normans in 1086, there were found to be less than two million.

During this period, the forests grew again, over the sites of ancient villages, over the splendid villas of the Romans, over the meadowland where there was no one to cultivate it. The marshlands reappeared as drainage ditches silted up, but the rivers remained open. It was up the rivers that the invading Danes and Saxons came. Their houses were rectangular and just as expendable as the circular huts of prehistory, but, with the gradual conversion of the whole country to Christianity, they began to build churches, always on a site that was already sacred. Some of the churches were built of stone; nearly all at least had stone foundations. And from this time the position of the village became fixed.

But if the village itself was clustered round, or centred on, the church, the disposition of villages in the countryside was more or less dictated by the system of agriculture. The 'infield', which was immediately around the village, was under constant cultivation, probably by now on the three-course system, while the 'outfield' was only cultivated at need and would have been used principally for grazing. In very rich lowland areas the outfield might have been about a mile from the village, so that villages would occur approximately every two miles. In poorer, hillier districts they were further apart.

It was the Saxons who introduced the system of strip farming. During the Roman occupation, cultivation seems to have been on the Iron Age pattern of small square fields, but the Saxons enlarged these fields and divided them into strips, each one about ten times as long as it was wide. The strips could then be operated on the three-course system – one down to winter-sown wheat or rye, one to spring-sown barley, oats, peas or beans, and one fallow – which was less wasteful than the Iron Age two-course system. The size of the strips may well have been dictated by the teams of six or sometimes eight oxen that drew the ploughs, as they, of course, had to be turned. Strips of this kind can still be seen in parts of the Midlands.

The Norman kings accepted the Saxon land divisions and the Saxon social system. They planted huge forests in which to hunt and enclosed vast tracts of land for this

THWAITE, NORTH YORKSHIRE

The little grey cottages of the village of Thwaite were once inhabited by the lead miners of Swaledale. For centuries large quantities of lead were produced here and legend has it that some was even sent, in Herod's day, to Rome and Jerusalem. Thwaite was the birthplace of two naturalist brothers, Richard and Cherry Kearton. They achieved fame in the 1920s and 30s, producing a large number of books and films and giving broadcast talks. From Thwaite the Buttertubs Pass leads upwards to a height of some 1600 feet with Lovely Seat on the left and the Great Shunner Fell on the right before dropping down into Wensleydale. In times gone past the folk of Swaledale or Swardill as it is called locally, thought nothing of the nine- or ten-mile walk over the pass to the market town of Hawes.

purpose. Around the villages we may suppose that woodland and copses were carefully preserved, as pigs could be fed in them and wood collected for burning and for repairing tools and houses. The countryside was occasionally ravaged by civil war, but the thirteenth century, in particular, seems to have been one of continuing agricultural prosperity. With territorial divisions increasingly guaranteed by laws that were increasingly enforced, hedges could be planted or dry-stone walls built between the fields.

Then, in 1348, came the Black Death – bubonic plague carried by fleas: human fleas, dog fleas, black rat fleas. In little more than a year the population was reduced by three-quarters, or two-thirds, or a half, or a third, or a twentieth, depending on which book you read. Landlords were unable to find labour to till their fields and began to put them down to grass for sheep, since a flock could be tended by one man. The fields grew larger and the woodlands were extended. The large quantities of wool produced were to be the basis of the enormous wealth of England in the fifteenth century; the trees were used to build the Tudor and Elizabethan navies, founders of a great maritime empire.

But some villages disappeared. Still made of mud and straw, still without stone foundations and with very few inhabitants, the ground closed over them. Sometimes they were moved deliberately. An early example of this occurred in 1579 when Sir Christopher Hatton – whose money came principally from foreign trade and who gave his name to Hatton Garden, in London – wished to build a handsome mansion at Holdenby, in Northamptonshire. He chose a site between two villages. The lower one was swept away to make a large and elaborate garden; the upper village was demolished and rebuilt round a square green as part of the garden plan. There were arches in the garden walls through which this village could be seen.

The great work of the seventeenth century was the draining of the Fens and the dredging of rivers, continuing the work left off by the Romans more than a thousand years before. The last battle to be fought on English soil took place on Sedgemoor in 1685, then recently drained and where, in our day, very ancient trackways have been discovered. By the beginning of the eighteenth century there was probably as much land under grass or the plough as there had been two thousand years before.

It was the eighteenth century that completed the landscape as we know it today. The great enclosures, frequently of common land, which went on between 1730 and

1840, by private Enclosure Acts, fixed most of the fields at their present size, though many fields retain their size and shape from the Saxon era. The great houses were placed in the middle of large parks, and vast woodlands were planted, partly to screen the houses from the public gaze. If a village, or a cottage, got in the way then it was removed, usually, it is only fair to say, being rebuilt elsewhere. These were the forerunners of the estate villages of the nineteenth century, built by enlightened landlords who had discovered the conditions in which their labourers lived. One of the earlier 'moved' villages can still be seen in Dorset today. When rebuilt it consisted of a double row of identical semi-detached cottages, painted white and thatched, with a chestnut tree planted between each one, following the winding course of the village street. It must be considered as a model for much of the ribbon development of the 1930s. Gradually, the landscape no longer belonged to the village, as it had originally done. The village was now more an object within it.

But the most important event was the Agricultural Revolution of the 1730s, the invention of the four-course system, that is to say growing wheat one year, a root crop the next, barley the next and clover the year after that, in continuous rotation so that the ground never lies fallow. The seed drill was also invented at this time so that now far less seed was wasted – it had previously been sown broadcast. Food production soared and there was a renewed demand for wool. Perhaps, in those country villages just before the Industrial Revolution, everyone had enough to eat.

The canals, constructed at the end of the century, and the railways, in the middle of the next one, did alter the landscape to an extent, though they were inserted into the countryside with a skill that seems to elude our motorway engineers, but they did not change the villages. Where a canal touched an existing village, it might grow larger; where a railway went to a village, it might become a town. Mostly the villages were left to slumber and crumble, through boom and gloom, until discovered by the hikers and bikers of the 1930s and the motorists of the 1960s.

So, as you picnic by a stone wall in the Cotswolds, as you wander down a leafy lane in Sussex, or stride across a grassy down, or gallop over heathy moorland, or even clamber in the Lake District, remember those ancient axe-makers, drovers, ditchers, ploughmen, woodmen, hedgers and shepherds. It was they who gave you what you see.

HALLSANDS, DEVON

Hallsands is one of England's lost villages. In the nineteenth century it was a flourishing fishing village, with twenty cottages and an inn strung along a village street parallel with the sea. In 1917, an enormous amount of shingle was dredged offshore for building work in Devonport, to support the War Effort. In some places the beach was lowered by as much as fifteen feet, leaving a rock stack known as Wilson's Rock standing alone. The village, no longer protected from the tides by its bank of shingle, began to be washed away and a fierce gale in that same year completed its destruction.

BLAKENEY, NORFOLK

Blakeney, together with Wiveton and Cley-next-the-Sea, was an important port in the sixteenth and seventeenth centuries, bringing coal, salt, Flemish bricks and timber to north-eastern Norfolk. The major export was corn from its great grain fields. Blakeney alone continued as a commercial port – chiefly for the carrying of coal – until the beginning of this century. Indeed, it still continues as a harbour, now for pleasure boats, and it is an important centre for sailing. The village is small and mostly built of flint with brick dressings. It was originally centred on a Carmelite House, founded in 1296, but this is now merely a fragmentary ruin. The quay overlooks the marshes and, in summer, is crowded with sailing boats of every sort and kind.

SALTHOUSE, NORFOLK

Salthouse on the north Norfolk coast was, like its neighbours Blakeney, Wiveton and Cley-next-the-Sea, a port since the Middle Ages. The reclamation of the salt marshes, which put an end to the port, has provided an ideal habitat for wading birds of every kind. Even more than Cley, Salthouse is known to 'twitchers' (bird-watchers) throughout the world and it is here, in the local café, that they congregate in the season to wait for news of rare-bird sightings. The large church of St Nicholas is placed on an eminence, broadside on to the sea. It is almost entirely Perpendicular in style and was completed in 1513. Just inland from the village is Salthouse Heath, a rather desolate area, overgrown with bracken and gorse that hide a collection of Bronze Age tumuli.

OARE, SOMERSET

Doone Valley, as it is popularly called, is near the village of Oare on Exmoor. This was the setting of the famous novel *Lorna Doone* by R.D.Blackmore. He is supposed to have written part of the book at Parsonage Farm where he set one of the Doone raids. The path from Malmshead along Badgworthy Water passes a plaque erected in 1969 to commemorate the centenary of the publication of the novel.

OARE, SOMERSET

This small church of St Mary was used as the setting for the dramatic marriage of John Ridd and Lorna Doone. It was through one of the windows of the old chancel that she was shot on her wedding day. Blackmore's grandfather was rector here and the novel is set in and around Oare on the northern slopes of Exmoor. Although it was first published in 1869 the novel has never lost its popularity; as well as telling a stirring tale, the book describes the Exmoor countryside in loving detail. So much so, indeed, that visitors from all parts of the world come to Oare with the hope of identifying such places as Plovers Barrow Farm, the home of the hero, John, or, as he was called, Jan Ridd.

SHARRINGTON, NORFOLK

Magnificent 'skyscapes',
typical of the great flat lands
of East Anglia, have been
the inspiration of many
remarkable English landscape
painters from Constable
onwards. The very openness of
the country gives a special
quality to the light and the
little village of Sharrington, in
north-east Norfolk, is seen to
advantage across a field of ripe
corn. The relative absence of
rainfall and the undulating
nature of the land have made
the eastern counties renowned
for both the quantity and the
quality of their grain harvests.
The church of All Saints at
Sharrington dates from the
thirteenth century, reminding
one that prosperity came early
to north Norfolk.

SAXTEAD GREEN, SUFFOLK

This fine post-mill at Saxtead
Green in east Suffolk was in
use until 1947. It is probable
that there has been a mill on
the site since about 1300, but
the earliest reference to this
one was in 1706. We also know
that, in 1796, the miller's name
was Amos Webber. The round
house at the base contains the
mill stones; the body
containing the machinery, and
carrying the sails, rotates on
this. The fantail at the rear
keeps the sails square into the
wind. Saxtead Green is about a
mile from the village and
church of Saxtead – a broad,
grassed area straddling an old
Roman road, which once
provided grazing for the
nearby farms and cottages. The
most interesting survival of
these is the Manor Farm, on
what was once a completely
moated site. The house itself
dates from the mid fifteenth
century, but the moat is
certainly earlier.

PORT ISAAC, CORNWALL

Port Isaac was the main fishing village in the Bay of Port Isaac, guarded on the west by The Rumps, and on the east by the great headland of Tintagel. For centuries villages such as Port Isaac, in Cornwall, made their living from the great herring and pilchard shoals. Evidence of this can still be seen in the old fish cellars where fish was salted down and stored for export all over the south of England from Tudor times until this century. When, for some unaccountable reason, the herring and the pilchard deserted Cornish waters, in the 1930s, it was reckoned that one out of every four boats was either sold or laid up. Much hardship resulted, but now Port Isaac, with its steep irregular street and red and white cottages is a holiday resort. In the high season it is almost impossible to move and traffic is a definite hazard.

PORT ISAAC, CORNWALL

The windswept cliffs and headlands round Port Isaac in north Cornwall are now, thankfully, protected by the National Trust. The work of the developer along other stretches of this coast is not a thing of beauty. Fortunately, some parts of the village itself are also owned by the National Trust. Despite its tremendous popularity as a holiday area, Port Isaac has managed to retain its truly Cornish character.

LITTLE BARRINGTON, GLOUCESTERSHIRE

Little Barrington lies in the valley of the Windrush, perhaps the most charming of Cotswold streams; it rises at Temple Guiting, meanders through Bourton-on-the-Water, passes the Barringtons, Burford and Witney to debouch eventually into the Thames. The sister village of Great Barrington lies on the north side of the river and it is from here that stone from the Barrington quarry was shipped all over the county. There is an old sloping stone weir at Little Barrington that dates from the seventeenth century and that was made to help the stone-carrying barges of that time. The village itself centres on a triangular green through which flows a stream; this and the Cotswold stone houses and cottages surrounding it present an idyllic village scene.

SWINBROOK, OXFORDSHIRE

There were medieval vineyard terraces near Swinbrook, a charmingly sheltered village on the banks of the Windrush. About 1920, the second Lord Redesdale built a fairly ugly house on a hill above, to contain his interesting family. This was to include two writers, Nancy and Jessica Mitford, the present Duchess of Devonshire and two notable Fascist ladies, Diana, for many years the second wife of the late Sir Oswald Mosley, and Unity, for some time a close friend and associate of the late Adolf Hitler. She broke off this connection at the outbreak of war in 1939 and a German bomb, locally reputed to have been aimed at Unity, was duly dropped on Swinbrook in 1940. It destroyed some of the stained glass in the church but left undamaged the superb Fettiplace monuments, dating from 1613 and 1686.

GLANDFORD, NORFOLK

Glandford lies between Bayfield and Cley in north Norfolk. The whole village was built at the beginning of the twentieth century by Sir Alfred Jodrell of Bayfield Hall, who even rebuilt the church using medieval materials. Bayfield Hall itself has one of the most beautiful parks in Norfolk. It was begun in the eighteenth century, when it was described as 'grandly rural in an eminent degree', and lies on the river Glaven, which was widened to make a long, slender lake. The final landscaping was finished about 1830. The house was described at this time as standing 'on broken ground, which swells and falls in easy slopes'. The small valley in which Glandford is situated is equally beautiful and the village has been most sympathetically placed, the flint and brick harmonizing perfectly with the landscape.

DUDDINGTON, NORTHAMPTONSHIRE

This is the river Welland that forms the boundary between what was once Rutland, now Leicestershire, and Northamptonshire. The stone bridge was probably built in the fourteenth century but has been very much altered since; the building just beyond is a seventeenth-century water mill. Nearly all the houses in the village are stone and roofed with stone slates – hardly surprising as Collyweston is only a mile or so to the north. It is here that the frosting process of splitting stone roofing slates was developed – it became an industry around 1600, but this method was certainly used by the Romans. The quarried slabs of stone are laid out in cold weather and watered constantly, especially at dusk, and the expansion of the water as it turns to ice in the laminations splits the stone into slates. These then have only to be shaped, dressed and holed.

SELWORTHY, SOMERSET

Selworthy, in west Somerset, is on a steep hill on the fringe of Exmoor, giving it magnificent views of Dunkery Beacon and the heathery moorland. The village itself consists of pretty whitewashed cottages and is approached along a romantic lane almost enclosed by holly, oak and ash trees. The church of All Saints is renowned for the beauty of the south aisle, which is quite extraordinarily lavish for a village church. The waggon roof, so named for the resemblance to the inside of the canvas tilts over waggons, is decorated with angels holding shields; the beautiful, carved bosses show the face of Christ and the symbols of the Passion. Also in the church is a pair of monuments by the great nineteenth-century sculptor, Chantrey. They commemorate two members of the Dyke Acland family. It was Thomas Dyke Acland who, early in the nineteenth century, built the village as we know it today.

TIVINGTON, SOMERSET

The tiny village of Tivington looks across the valley of Horner Water to the great broad sweeps of Exmoor, which is shared between Somerset and Devon. Although officially called Exmoor Forest, the Commissioners, who surveyed it for the Crown around the year 1800, reported only thirty-seven trees still standing. Many have been the schemes to bring prosperity to Exmoor, among them two rather abortive attempts at iron mining and many farming ventures. Today, however, the bare moorland is chiefly thought of as a holiday area. The little chapel of St Leonard has had a curious history; for some time it served as a school but is now, again, a church. It is attached to one side of the cottage that was once the priest's house.

EDALE, DERBYSHIRE

Edale, in the northernmost part of Derbyshire, is a small village of strong, solid, extremely well-built houses, most of them from the eighteenth century or later. It has an inn, a shop and a café and is one of the few villages in England still with a railway station at which the trains actually stop. The houses are made of the local, very hard millstone grit and are roofed with slate. It is the centre of a district of small farming communities and behind it, to the north, is some of the wildest and most desolate country in England, leading up to Kinder Scout, more usually known as The Peak. It is a wilderness of rough grass and damp moss, naked peat and naked rock, which extends along the tops of the Pennines all the way to Scotland. It is a hard country, hostile and uncompromising, of interest principally to hikers and photographers.

EDALE, DERBYSHIRE

The Pennine Way, a 270-mile-long footpath along the tops of the Pennines, which starts at Grindsbrook Booth in this village of Edale, was established in 1965. It is a memorial to the vision of Mr Tom Stephenson, who began to work for the formation of a pedestrian right of way along the whole length of the Pennines, south to north, as early as 1935. Thirty years of careful and patient discussion with the numerous landowners, both public and private, were to follow. Now that it is established, Edale has become, in the summer, crowded, almost noisy. The first section of the walk ends at Kinder Downfall, by way of Grindsbrook Clough. Over the Grinds Brook itself there is an ancient, narrow packhorse bridge, indicating that the village is older than it might at first appear.

EAST NORTON, LEICESTERSHIRE

The small village of East Norton lies on the road between Uppingham and Leicester, just near the old border between Leicestershire and the now extinct Rutland. This distant view of the village in the open landscape is essentially English and typical of these small, unremarkable villages lying on the upland plain almost in the centre of the whole country. Next to the village is Keythorpe Hall, a house that belonged, in the nineteenth century, to Lord Berners. He once appeared at a dinner held at Tugby, the next village, dressed in a coat made of wool which that morning had been growing on the back of one of his sheep at Keythorpe. The other notable house nearby is Launde Abbey, built on the ruins of an Augustinian Priory. The property was granted to Thomas Cromwell at the Dissolution but he never lived there. It was his son, Gregory, who married a sister of Queen Jane Seymour, who did live in the mansion.

HARTSOP, CUMBRIA

Sheep are an indigenous part of the Cumbrian scene. The Swaledale and the Herdwick are the two most famous local breeds; both so hardy that they can live out on the fells in almost any weather. The name Herdwick is a medieval word for a sheep fold or farm on the hills but there are many romantic stories of the origins of these sheep: that they swam ashore from a ship of the Spanish Armada, that they were brought by the Vikings, and so on. But whatever their origins they are so firmly linked with Cumbria that the words sheep and Herdwick are almost synonymous here. Behind the snow-covered field is the village of Hartsop.

HARTSOP, CUMBRIA

The road from Penrith to Windermere skirts the west side of Ullswater and, at Patterdale, begins to ascend, passing this remote village of Hartsop. The road rises steadily from the head of Ullswater for about five miles until it reaches the Kirkstone Pass and then descends to Troutbeck and the better-known Windermere. It is from Patterdale, just a mile or two from Hartsop that the ascent of Helvellyn by the south route is generally attempted. This is the most popular route. Cumbria and the Lake District in particular is well known to both walkers and climbers and, in the season, is busy with both.

GRANGE, CUMBRIA

The double bridge, with a grassy island between the arches, is at Grange in Borrowdale. From here the river Derwent flows down into Derwent Water itself. Borrowdale is part of the unique volcanic landscape of the Lake District. The volcanic rock provides some of the world's finest roofing slates; those from the Borrowdale-Buttermere group of quarries are an extraordinary brilliant green colour. Mining has been an important industry in the fells from Roman times. Queen Elizabeth I even imported workers from Germany and by 1567 furnaces were at work near Keswick smelting iron ore. The famous graphite mine is higher up Borrowdale at Seathwaite; this was used in the eighteenth century for casting cannon balls but later for the lead pencil industry centred at Keswick.

WITHYPOOL, SOMERSET

Withypool nestles in the valley of the river Barle on Exmoor and is still basically an agricultural community. Farming is the main industry here although tourism also plays an important part in the village life of west Somerset. The mainly pale, colour-washed cottages and farmhouses are roofed with grey Devonian slate. The whole of what is now Somerset was intensively colonized during the Bronze Age – from about 1500 to 800 BC – and, at Withypool, there is one of the stone circles dating from that time with thirty-seven stones still standing. Just a few miles down the Barle is Tarr Steps, where the river is crossed by an immense clapper bridge. It is of seventeen spans, 180 feet long and one of the finest in the country.

ARNCLIFF, NORTH YORKSHIRE

This parish church of St Oswald is at Arncliff. It is the largest of the four villages in Littledale and is watered by the Skirfare river. It was Arncliff that provided some of the inspiration for Charles Kingsley's classic children's book, *The Water Babies*. Kingsley was staying at nearby Malham Tarn House and walked over to Arncliff to have tea with a Miss Elizabeth Hammond; she appeared in the book as the 'woman in the red petticoat'. When the chimney-boy hero, Tom, slips into the water to join the other water babies it was, supposedly, here at Arncliff and the river was the Skirfare. The best way to approach Arncliff is from Settle by the high road across Fountains Fell. The views are quite spectacular before the road drops down into Littledale.

STAITHES, NORTH YORKSHIRE

The fishing village of Staithes is on the coast of North Yorkshire with only the Shetland Islands between it and the Arctic, some thousand miles away to the north. The natural harbour is sheltered by two headlands – the nearby Boulby Head, at 600 feet is the highest in England. These rather forbidding cliffs are formed of clay and erosion presents a serious problem – Staithes is constantly retreating inland. The Cod and Lobster Inn has been washed away three times and at the last inundation hundreds of bottles of beer were seen bobbing out to sea – a terrible sight.

STAITHES, NORTH YORKSHIRE

Captain Cook lived in Staithes for eighteen months working for a Mr William Sanderson, a grocer and haberdasher. He was born the son of a farm labourer who lived at nearby Great Ayton and it was his employer, Squire Skottowe, who apprenticed the young James to Mr Sanderson. Sadly, the shop on the front has been washed away but the cottage where he lived, in Church Street, forms part of the Captain Cook Heritage Trail from his birthplace, Marton, to Whitby. In his day this was one of the most important ports in England and it was from here that he made his first sea voyage – in a collier. His statue in Whitby is inscribed: 'To strive, to seek, to find and not to yield'. This famous son of Yorkshire must be one of the greatest examples of coming 'up from nowt'.

❖ PHOTOGRAPHIC NOTES ❖

My aim while taking the photographs was to create a timeless atmosphere, so that the villages could be seen as they may have been at the turn of the century, before the petrochemical age changed most of England beyond recognition. One gets hints of what this England may have been like from tinted Victorian and Edwardian postcards or from the work of contemporary photographers, such as Frank Meadow Sutcliffe's evocative pictures of Whitby.

There is a wonderful description of the tranquillity of English rural life by John Cowper Powys in his book *Wolf Solent*, written in the 1920s. On seeing a cow tethered in Basingstoke churchyard, he writes:

> 'For the space of a quarter of a minute he watched this cow, it gathered to itself such an invisible placidity that its feet seemed planted in a green pool that was older than time itself.'

I wonder what Cowper Powys would have made of Basingstoke today – mile upon mile of faceless, sterile architecture that is echoed around London, in Swindon, Stevenage and Milton Keynes. It is this world that has invaded the villages of England, making the job of photography extremely difficult.

The first problem is parked cars, which date the photograph. For this reason I had to exclude from the book some of the most attractive villages in the country. After the problem of cars, and this is not always insurmountable because people did move their cars for me (I would like to thank all those people for making the photographs possible!), the next problem is the new doors and windows syndrome. With the advent of double glazing and new plastic and aluminium doors and windows, many people have torn out the original Victorian sash windows and replaced them, sadly, with windows totally inappropriate to the age and design of the buildings. The effect is very frustrating when photographing rows of cottages – instead of forming a harmonious group one of these unfortunate buildings can make photography impossible.

Another sanitizing effect that has come with the advent of the second home and the replacement of the original inhabitants, is a preponderance of plastic paint, porches, garden gnomes, wheelbarrows with flowers planted in them, and cartwheels on walls! This is, however, not true of every village and in some one can still find something of the England of Cowper Powys and Frank Meadow Sutcliffe.

My quest for this lost England took me to nearly every corner of the country and at times I was well rewarded for my travels. I tried mostly to work in the morning and evening when the light is at its best, staying overnight in places that I hoped would produce good morning shots, and arriving at possible locations in the evening before sunset. One of the problems of working like this is that unless one has unlimited time to stay in one spot, one has to take what one can get at whatever end of the day one arrives, while the other side of the street, as it were, remains neglected.

Shooting into a low sun is usually unsuccessful, unless you are some way off from the subject, and as many villages are surrounded by new bungalows and asbestos barns the village nestling in the landscape that remains photographable is rare indeed.

I used a Canon F.1. 35 mm camera with a 28 mm lens for most of the photographs, and occasionally, when I felt the need for a larger format, a 6 × 7 Pentax with a 50 mm lens. There is a little more subtlety of colour and tone in the larger-format transparency, and this was useful when I had a wide expanse of sky or a particularly subtle light. With the 6 × 7 I used Ektachrome 64 or 100 ASA transparency film with an 81A filter to warm the tones a little. On the 35 mm camera I used Kodachrome 64 ASA with the same filter. Several of the more distant shots were taken with a 90 mm lens on the 35 mm format, or with a 135 mm lens on the 6 × 7 cm format, also using an 81A filter. Occasionally it was necessary to use graduated filters to enhance the atmosphere, but when doing this I have always endeavoured to use the colour nearest to the prevailing sky colour, so as not to cause too much colour distortion.

One of the difficulties of photographing groups of buildings or streets from the ground, on a wide-angle lens, is the problem of converging vertical lines. I usually managed to overcome this by rigging my tripod up on top of my car, which has, fortunately, a very solid roof. The same solution could be achieved with a step ladder and an extended tripod.

I used a small aperture for most of the photographs so that the depth of field would be adequate to keep sharp both the buildings in the foreground and those at infinity; this, of course, meant using a tripod all the time, because the light was usually quite low necessitating rather long exposures.

Although the changes that have taken place in most villages over the last few years have made photography much more difficult, and although the photographer, more than other artists, has to depend on and deal with what is actually there, I hope that the previous pages will show that many English villages remain unspoilt and that this will encourage the householder to reflect a little, not only on his own house or cottage, but to see it in harmony with its surroundings before allowing the salesman or builder to talk him into something irrevocable.

✤ BIBLIOGRAPHY ✤

AA Book of British Villages, Drive Publications, Basingstoke, 1980

Banks, F. R. *English Villages*, Batsford, London, 1963; Hastings House, New York, 1964

Benfield, Eric *Dorset*, Robert Hale, London, 1950

Berry, Claude *Portrait of Cornwall*, Robert Hale, London, 1963

Black's Guide to Leicestershire and Rutland, Adam & Charles Black, London, 1884

Brabant, P. G. *Oxfordshire*, Methuen, London, 1919

Brunskill, R. W. *Traditional Buildings of Britain*, Gollancz, London, 1981

Church, Richard *Kent*, Robert Hale, London, 1948

Colvin, H. M. *Biographical Dictionary of English Architects*, John Murray, London, 1954; Harvard University Press, Cambridge MA., 1954

Cox, Charles J. *Gloucestershire*, Methuen, London, 1949

Cox, Charles J. *The Little Guides: Hampshire*, Methuen, London, 1929; revised by R. L. P. Jowitt, Batsford London, 1949

Darley, Gillian *Built in Britain*, Weidenfeld & Nicolson, London, 1983

Davidson, Robin *Cornwall*, Batsford, London, 1978

Eagle, Dorothy and Carnell, Hilary *The Oxford Literary Guide to the British Isles*, Oxford University Press, Oxford and New York, 1977

Finberg, Josceline *The Cotswolds*, Eyre Methuen, London, 1977

Fleming, Laurence and Gore, Alan *The English Garden*, Michael Joseph, London, 1979

Haines, George H. *Shropshire and Herefordshire Villages*, Robert Hale, London, 1974

Handbook for Travellers in Oxfordshire, John Murray, London, 1894

Heath, Frank R. *Dorset*, Methuen, London, 1949

Heath, Frank R. *Wiltshire*, Methuen, London, 1925; 7th edition Batsford, London, 1949

Honeyman, Herbert L. *Northumberland*, Robert Hale, London, 1949

James Herriot's Yorkshire, Michael Joseph, London, 1979; St Martin's Press, New York, 1981

Jewson, Norman *By Chance I did Rove*, Richard Courtalt, Stroud, 1973

Little, Bryan *Portrait of Somerset*, Robert Hale, London, 1969

Marshall, J. D. *Portrait of Cumbria*, Robert Hale, London, 1981

Mee, Arthur *Cornwall*, Hodder & Stoughton, London, 1967

Mee, Arthur *Gloucestershire*, Hodder & Stoughton, London, 1950; new edition 1966

Mee, Arthur *Hertfordshire*, Hodder & Stoughton, London, 1965

Mee, Arthur *Leicestershire and Rutland*, Hodder & Stoughton, London, 1967

Mee, Arthur *Northumberland*, Hodder & Stoughton, London, 1952

Mee, Arthur *Somerset*, Hodder & Stoughton, London, 1968

Mee, Arthur *Yorkshire North Riding*, Hodder & Stoughton, London, 1941

Muir, Richard *The English Village*, Thames & Hudson, London, 1980

Nicholson, Norman *Cumberland and Westmorland*, Robert Hale, London, 1949; Macmillan, New York, 1949

Olivier, Edith *Wiltshire*, Robert Hale, London, 1951

Pakington, Humphrey *English Villages and Hamlets*, privately published, 1934; Scribner, New York, 1935

Parker, Rowland *The Common Stream*, Collins, London, 1975

Pevsner, Nikolaus *The Buildings of England*, 46 vols., Penguin, London and New York, 1951–74

Sandon, Eric *Suffolk Houses*, Baron Publishing, Woodbridge, 1977

Sharp, Thomas *Northumberland and Durham*, Shell Guide Series, Faber, London, 1938

Taylor, Christopher *Village and Farmstead, A History of Rural Settlement in England*, George Philip, London, 1983; Sheridan House, New York, 1983

Tompkins, Herbert W. *Hertfordshire*, Methuen, London, 1903

Treasures of Britain, Drive Publications, Basingstoke, 1968

Trewin, J. C. (Ed.) *The West Country Book*, Webb & Bower, Exeter, 1981

Waite, Vincent *Portrait of the Quantocks*, Robert Hale, London, 1964

Wilts and Dorset Murray's Handbook, John Murray, London, 1899

Witts, The Rev. F. E. *The Diary of a Cotswold Parson* (Edited by David Verey), Alan Sutton, Gloucester, 1978

Wood, G. Bernard *Yorkshire*, Batsford, London, 1968

Wood, G. Bernard *Yorkshire Tribute*, Methuen, London, 1950

Yaxley, David *Portrait of Norfolk*, Robert Hale, London, 1977